This is Your Life — *Write It!*

Leave Legacy Footprints

Leona Choy

This is Your Life — *Write It!*

Leave Legacy Footprints

Leona Choy

Golden Morning Publishing
Winchester, Virginia

Unless otherwise indicated, all Scripture references are from the New American Standard Bible, Copyright © 1960, 1962, 1963, 1968, 1971, 1972, 1973, 1975, 1977 The Lockman Foundation. Used by permission.

This is Your Life—*Write It! Leave Legacy Footprints*

© 2002 Leona Choy

Published by *Golden Morning Publishing*
P.O. Box 2697, Winchester, VA 22604

Produced by Richard Choy

All rights reserved. No part of this publication may be reproduced, stored in a retrieval system, or transmitted, in any form or by any means, electronic, mechanical, photocopying, recording, or otherwise, without the prior written permission of the publisher, except for brief quotations in reviews or articles.

Library of Congress Cataloging-in-Publication Data

Choy, Leona
       This is Your Life—*Write It! Leave Legacy Footprints*

Library of Congress Control Number: 2002094215
ISBN 1-889283-17-7
       1. Non-fiction—Writing Instruction—Memoirs
         Includes bibliographical references

Printed in the United States by:
Morris Publishing
3212 East Highway 30
Kearney, NE 68847
1-800-650-7888

Published in the United States of America

Contents

This is Your Life—*Write it!*
Leave Legacy Footprints

Introduction *"Trunk" Destiny*.. vii

1. Find Your Direction *Enjoy the Journey!*........................ 1

2. Target Your Readership *Build Generational Bridges*..... 9

3. Generous Benefits *Surprise Bonuses*............................. 19

4. Shorties of Significance *Characteristics of Memoirs*..... 31

5. Memory Triggers *Interview Yourself*............................. 41

6. Enhance Your Content *Select Significant Extras*........... 49

7. Get Ready, Get Set, GO! *The Writing Process*............... 61

8. Dig for Gold *Search and Research*................................ 71

9. Wrap It Up *The Final Touch*... 83

10. To Market—To Market? *Polish and Package*............... 95

    Resources.. 110
    Endnotes... 112
    About the Author.. 114

Introduction

"Trunk" Destiny

As a part of your family tree, you start out as a tiny bud that grows into a little twig. Then you develop into a branch. As the years go by, you become a trunk with your own branches which, in turn, sprout buds and little twigs. Your branches become trunks and eventually, inevitably, *you become a part of the root system.* Future members of your family may eagerly research *your life* to find out vital facets of their heritage.

Will you make it easy or difficult for them? It is up to you.

In my autobiography, *Czeching My Roots*, I titled the first chapter, *What's in "the trunk."* I put my life story in perspective in a poem I wrote.

TRUNK DESTINY

I have roots and also branches.
I am part of what has been
and what is yet to be.
In between is *me:*
the *trunk* of the family tree.

Through me pass
generations from antiquity
who have determined

what I have become.
They are my history.
They have molded me.

From me new branches spring.
They are my posterity.
Some choice I have
to assist and incline them
toward the best
of what they might become.
Still, they are free
to grow and change
within the range
of their heredity and opportunity
and God's special plan
arranged from Eternity.

For me, the trunk between,
I pray that I might be a planting
strong against the inevitable storms
yet bending with the wind
passing on the best
from roots unseen
yet giving branches room
to stretch and reach
upward to new heights
because I fulfilled
with the help of God
my trunk destiny.[1]

I challenge you, as I challenged myself when I began writing my life story: Will you fulfill your *trunk destiny* while you can? Will your posterity really know who you were and what the times were like when you were young? If you are getting on in years, do your children and grandchildren realize that you were not always a parent, not always a grandma or grandpa? You had, and still have, hopes, dreams, ideals, ideas, problems, and struggles just like they have. Don't you want them to know the *real you*? An entire human forest may grow up around your family tree. Do you want to be lost in that forest by failing to pass on your inner, unique identity to those who follow you? You have lived. You matter.

Families differ in their regard for the past. Blessed are you if your parents and grandparents poured into you the wonderful stories of your heritage. You have a head start. Appreciate your treasure and record it for your posterity. When I started looking into my heritage, I was disappointed that my parents and grandparents left no letters, diaries, records or even anything in their own handwriting about themselves or their roots. They *passed on* without *passing on* anything tangible of our heritage. They lived and left. I had only my personal, imperfect memories of them, some of which may be colored by my perceptions more than reality. They could have spoken for themselves even after they left, but they didn't. I guess they were too busy living and making a living. Now one or two or three generations separate us. I had to dig in hard ground to find out anything about my ancestry. Like an eager detective, I followed slim clues to see if they would lead anywhere.

I had no idea what a rich heritage treasure I possessed until I started digging. I was amazed, surprised, delighted, and excited with every small gem of the past that I discovered. No matter how hard I dig, I will never be able to recover some parts of our precious heritage treasure to share with our posterity.

It was not all because of their shortcoming, however. When I was young, it didn't even occur to me to ask about our ancestry or my parents' or grandparents' earlier years. I didn't really care then, but I certainly did later. How I regret my thoughtlessness!

Your family members, especially the younger generations, may not seem to care right now either. Be that as it may, I suggest that it is *your* responsibility to prepare for later when they *will* care. It is up to you to *fulfill your trunk destiny* and pass on the essence of yourself and what you know of your priceless past.

What is ahead in this book?

My purpose in this book is threefold.

First, I hope to motivate you to write your own life story with realism and candor, to share yourself with your family, descendants and friends honestly and meaningfully. You may never have thought about doing that. On the other hand, you may always have wanted to. Perhaps someone suggested, "You really *should* write your story." Perhaps your family is urging you to do so. In another chapter I will talk about the rich rewards of such writing for you and your descendants.

Second, I will provide some practical guidelines for writing the story of your life. It doesn't matter whether you are an inexperienced writer or a published author, you are already qualified simply because you have lived. No one knows your story better than you.

Whatever you write is sure to be interesting to your family and those who know you, but you want to write it as well as you can. You can find guidelines for good writing in other books on style, composition and grammar, so I will not duplicate those. To give you a start in the right direction, I will offer specific principles and approaches for writing memoirs.

Third, since I wrote and published my own autobiography and taught workshops to help others start writing theirs, I will let you in on how I did it. As we go along, I will give examples from my own book. It is certainly not because the way that I did it is the only way to write it, perhaps not even the best way, but it is one way. Then I encourage you to go ahead and do it *your* way.

Everyone's memories are in a personal storehouse. There is no master key to unlock your memories, but I will offer some interesting ways to stimulate your recall and get your memory juices flowing. The past is gone, but you can bring it back and share it vividly not only with present but future readers.

I will share some simple ways that I did research and where it led me. That may provide you with some ideas and inspiration on how to go about your exploration.

I will overview for you the characteristics of memoir writing, different aspects of the writing process, and what you might include. You may want to cover only your life or go further and delve into the past in a search for your ancestral heritage. It is your choice.

I will offer various options for packaging or publishing your life story. You may want to write only a partial memoir of some aspect or time period of your life. You may be satisfied to compile your stories in a notebook or folder or some easy, manageable way and then make a few copies for your family or friends. If you do want to publish your memoir as a book, I will give you suggestions, cautions, opportunities and advantages about self-publishing. I will discuss distribution and marketing possibilities.

Writing your life story should be a delightful adventure not a labored, overwhelming task. No one will breathe down your neck and insist that you do it in a certain way or criticize your efforts. What's not to like? This is *your* life, you lived it your way, and you are free to write it your way.

As you write, keep looking in the mirror to ask yourself, *"Am I having fun yet?"* You better answer with an enthusiastic "YES!"

So let's get going!

1

Find Your Direction

Enjoy the Journey!

"Memoir fever" spreads

When public figures retire or leave political office, they often announce that they are going to write their memoirs. Not only people in the public eye, but grass roots, ordinary folks are putting down their recollections on paper or tape. War veterans, housewives, retirees, blue color workers and professional people of all ages are searching for their roots. Alex Haley sparked a revival of searching for generational roots with his famous book and movie, *Roots*. It is no wonder a magazine article carried the title, *"Memoir fever" proves infectious, sweeps the country.*

A general sense of restlessness permeates our modern culture. Fewer and fewer people these days still live in the place of their birth. Our Western society has a high rate of mobility with families moving all over the country. The disintegration of the family unit strongly contributes to many people feeling rootless.

Countless children are raised with only one parent and often without grandparents nearby to provide generational continuity. Because of multiple marriages and the proliferation of blended families, many children grow to adulthood without much stable family structure. Adopted children often have an unsatisfied longing to know who they really are genetically. People struggle against the feeling of being anonymous and disconnected in a crowded world where individuals are lost in the shuffle.

The popularity of the A&E "Biography" program, one of my TV favorites, is soaring. The byline "Every life is a story" strikes a common chord. People feel a certain satisfaction in following the whole sweep of some celebrity's or public figure's lifetime in one hour from birth to the present, including struggles and triumphs, failures and foibles. The viewer is drawn to think about his own life and realize that he has gone through a lot, and his life is a story too.

You don't have to be famous or noticed by society or have accomplished something great. You are special because you lived and survived. Most memoirs that ordinary folk write seldom reach beyond the family circle. To "go public" with one's own story is not usually the main reason for writing. People simply want to be remembered.

Others may want to leave behind their own version of events and control what posterity will know about them.

Writing a memoir validates your life. As you go back in time, you reconnect with people who are no longer living and places that may no longer be there as you experienced them. You relive certain eras of history that your family has no way of knowing about except through sterile history books. But you lived through them, and you were a part of local history.

Don't worry, when you start writing, you will usually remember a lot more than you think. One memory triggers another in a domino effect. As you think about your childhood or thumb through a photo album, (or those shoeboxes of photos that never did get on to neatly organized pages) you find yourself on the way to memory lane.

The big picture

The following definitions may clarify terms commonly used and give you some direction as you choose the right format for your story.

A *genealogy* usually takes the form of a chart and is not narrative writing of stories. It is an orderly record of one's ancestry dealing primarily with names and dates and relationships of persons in a family tree. It consists of bare facts and is, in a sense, a skeleton without flesh.

A *biography* is written about another person's life by someone else. It is usually about a somewhat noted or recognizable person and needs to be well researched and accurately presented. The person being written about is more important than the writer. Biographies are the most popular non-fiction reading today. I have written seven biographies, some of persons still living, some historical biographies for which I had to do extensive research.

An *autobiography* is written *by you* not by someone else. It is usually a factual, tidy chronology of your whole life and generally turns out to be a substantial book. It may include not only your story but ancestral research and generational stories and information. This kind of writing differs from a genealogy in that it puts interesting flesh on the bones. You bring those "dry bones" back to life by resurrecting the dead (your ancestors) through your story. You let them walk, talk, feel and grow again.

There are some variations depending on the writing ability of the one whose story it is. Some autobiographies are bylined "with" another writer. Sometimes the notation on the book cover is "as told to." Sometimes the book is "ghost written," that is, another skilled writer does the actual writing, but the story is presented from the first person "I" as if the person himself were writing it. This takes a special kind of writing skill because the writer has to "put on the skin" of the person whose story it is and carefully keep to his style of speech and vocabulary. The finished product shouldn't sound like the writer but must have the flavor of the original story teller. All these are legitimate literary devices and depend on the degree of another person's help.

I have written autobiographies for several people in each of the above formats. Several were the lives of people from different cultures or ethnic backgrounds who were limited in their skill of writing in English. Their stories probably would not have been written without my help.

When I wrote my husband's autobiography, it was a combination of all the above. Since I wrote it after his death, I used notes and letters he had written, tape recordings, documents, and recollections of events in which both of us participated. It was based on 46 years of marriage and ministry together.

Although I wrote it as if "by" him in the first person, I switched back and forth between some of his story telling and some of mine. I plausibly imagined my husband Ted saying, "You were there, Leona, so you tell this story." Then I inserted in the text the notation "Leona's turn." Having concluded my part of the story, I turned it back to him with "Ted resumes." In some sense, that was also my partial autobiography because of the events we lived through together.

A *memoir* is more personal and informal than an autobiography. It is less overwhelming to write and may or may not require much research on your part. It is based almost entirely on your own recollections. The word "memoir" refers to your book as a *whole*. It is your personal history and package of memories. You are saying, "This was *my* world as I saw it and lived it." Only you can write the intimate account that is a memoir.

The term "memoirs" refers to the *contents* of the book. You are recording your memories. The "memorist" refers to you, the *writer*.

Partial memoirs

You don't have to cover your entire life when you write a memoir. You may if you wish. Or you can go all the way back to stories about your ancestors. You can write a partial memoir that highlights a particular period or event.

Marjorie Holmes, for instance, wrote a partial memoir only about her growing up years in Storm Lake, Iowa. Much later she wrote another partial memoir about her life with her second husband. A retired teacher and artist wrote a partial memoir about her 50 years of traveling around the world with her chaplain husband. She wrote it from the unique viewpoint of the steamer trunk which she took along on all those travels and titled it "Fifty Journeys." The "writer" was a contrived entity, the trunk, purely from Leah Penner Hiebert's imagination. The author listed on the book jacket was "A. Trunk." She endowed the trunk with special human attributes including the ability to hear, see, remember and warmly understand human relationships. You can do just about anything that suits your fancy as you write your memoir.

My friend Dave Weston wrote a partial memoir about his military service in World War II. Several of my missionary friends wrote about selected years of their lives overseas. A retired medical doctor wrote only about his decades as a missionary and titled it "My Alaska Years."

I subtitled my book *A Heritage Saga and Autobiography* because I combined both my life story and my ancestry. It is also a personal memoir in every sense of the term. In fact, I started writing only a memoir and thought I would limit it to recollections of my life. As I followed clues and became more curious, even intrigued, about my unknown ancestry and what contributed to my life from the past, the scope of my writing kept expanding. Before I realized it, I was searching through history for my roots and following mysterious trails of my forefathers.

I am assuming for the purposes of this book that you'll start writing a memoir. If you never get further or don't want to go further, you will have made a wonderful contribution to your family. But the same thing may happen to you as happened to me, and your writing may keep expanding backward to include as much of your heritage as you can possibly dig up. You will find some helps for research in this book, if you decide to go in that direction.

Don't limit yourself, if suddenly your writing takes wings. Follow your heart. Follow your personal clues and by all means *enjoy the journey.*

I'm Not a Nobody!

My spirit is bursting for identity.
The world pressures my conformity
debasing my personality
championing uniformity.
I abhor the abnormality
of my struggle for individuality
as I stumble around to see
whether I have any destiny.
I feel swallowed up in the futility
of being just a facsimile of humanity.

But...
In God's eyes I'm special!
I'm not a nonentity!
Before I was born God predestined me
Calvary was designed to set me free
from Satan's captivity
and break me out of the mold of anonymity.

I'm not consigned to the monotony
of homogeneity and nothingness.
In Jesus, I'm not a generality.
What a discovery: I'm not a nobody!
I'm not generic! I'm really me!
Jesus knows my name! [1]

2
Target Your Readership

Build Generational Bridges

It is important for you to know from the start for whom you are writing. I suggest you write that down so you can visualize that person or persons while you are recalling your experiences. You might have one of your children or a grandchild in mind and direct your writing to him or her. I considered readership carefully in the *Preface* of my autobiography and realized that because of the broad scope of what I covered, I aimed at a multiple readership:

"I wrote for my *grown children and their spouses* who are busy with their own lives, careers, and families. Each of my children knows me in a unique way but only in part. We interact at different levels and through varied relationships. Reading my entire story, I hope they will be able to put some pieces together and know me better.

I wrote for my *grandchildren,* some of whom are still young children, others are young adults. When the young ones grow up, I may not be here. They may not remember me well or at all. But when they are mature enough to read this book, they will be able to know the real me and may come to know themselves better through me.

I wrote for my *generations yet unborn.* Future branches of our family tree will be able to know me through my story and get a taste of the times in which I and our ancestors lived.

I wrote for readers with *similar* backgrounds, experiences or heritage, or whose parents or grandparents could identify.

I wrote also for those to whom my life and times are entirely *unfamiliar.* I hope they will be interested in my personal "wonder years" and life in early 20th century.

I wrote for the wider readership of those interested in the *historical* aspects of my research.

I wrote for others who *search for meaning in life.* I hope that the account of my spiritual journey will inspire and encourage them toward a personal walk with God.

I wrote for people interested in *Christianity or missions or China.*

I wrote for those of *other ethnic or minority origins.* Because I rejected my ethnic background, they may identify with my struggle and come to value their unique ethnicity.

Finally, I realize it was important for me to write *for myself.* I needed to look at my life in its totality from the top of my present chronological mountain. It was enlightening to look back at my climb, all the way back to the foothills and even underground to the history of my forefathers. I wanted to trace with gratitude the loving hand of God in the details of my journey. *I am the one who benefited most from this writing."*

Most memorists will probably not have such multiple purposes for writing their life story. They may narrow down their potential readership to their family and friends. On the other hand, they may also incorporate some of the readers I aimed at. Visualize clearly for whom you are writing so it will keep your story focused.

Blood kin and blended families

How about the blended families in your family circle, of whom there are so many these days? How can you write about people to whom they have no blood connection without having them feel left out? I have precious grandchildren in that category. I addressed that in my first chapter titled *What's in 'the Trunk.'*

"My husband and I were the *trunk* of our *family tree* and our four sons, Richard, Clifford, Gary, and Jeff, are our natural *branches.* Our trunk is unique because it is made up of two people from two geographically and culturally separate root systems. My husband, Ted, was from the continent of Asia, from the ancient and historic land of China. My heritage is from the continent of Europe, from what is now the Czech Republic. We met and married on still another continent, North America, to which my forefathers came to seek a better life.

Some of our branches are offspring from our own biological trunk—authentic *Chinese Czechers*—our sons and some of our grandchildren. But we have enthusiastically welcomed the grafting of some new branches into our tree through extended family relationships by marriage, blended families and adoption. I embrace grafted branches, lovingly chosen, just as warmly as branches sprouting from our original trunk. They enrich our family tree and bear wonderful varieties of fruit that our original tree could not have produced."

Who cares about your story?

First of all, *you* do! You don't want to be forgotten, do you? By writing your story you are saying to the world: "Here I am. I have lived. I want you to know me. I want to tell you what I went through and how I felt about it." A memoir is not an ego trip. Don't be overly modest or, on the other hand, be afraid that you are bragging when you write about yourself. Don't sell yourself short. Tell about your life realistically yet with humility for the privilege of having lived.

Your family may or may not care at this very moment. They may be immersed in their daily lives and goals and relationships and give little thought to their past or to yours. Give them time. But don't wait around for their interest or appreciation before you write your life.

Some families care deeply and encourage or strongly urge you to write your memoirs. Either way, I hope you will make that strategic investment of your time and memory because it may be the most valuable gift you could give them. You are leaving them your footprints etched in black and white on paper. To quote further from the first chapter of my autobiography:

"Children rarely care about their roots when they see their more exciting futures stretching out seemingly open-end ahead of them. It doesn't seem to matter to youth where they came from. They are usually concerned only with where they are going after school tomorrow. I felt that way myself.

In your youth, you view every day up close, as through a microscope. Usually it takes the seasoning of life, the more mature years, before you think about and value your roots. Eventually you begin to see your life in a broader panorama, on a wider screen than you did in your youth. You can see further after you've climbed some of the higher hills of life and experienced the valleys between. You can look back over your shoulder to see where you've come from and forward to where you are going.

God handed me the baton in life's race only for my lifetime. Now I am responsible to pass it on to the next generation. The words of a song by Jon Mohr express it well for me:

Surrounded by so great a cloud of witnesses,
Let us run the race, not only for the prize;
But, as those who've gone before us,
Let us leave for those behind us
The heritage of faithfulness passed on through godly lives.

Oh, may all who come behind us find us faithful.
May the fire of our devotion light their way.
May the footprints that we leave lead them to believe,
And the lives we live inspire them to obey.
Oh, may all who come behind us find us faithful." [1]

Who else cares? *God cares.*

If you are a Christian, God considers you a steward of the experiences He brought you through and of what He taught you through them. He has given you a spiritual mandate to pass on those things. It is also your opportunity and wonderful privilege. Several verses from the Bible set the stage for your spiritual motivation. King David of Israel, the writer of many of the Psalms, prayed and declared the following:

> "O God, You have been my hope, my confidence since my youth. From birth I have relied upon You. You brought me forth from my mother's womb. I will always praise You. Since my youth, O God, You have taught me, and to this day I declare Your marvelous deeds. Even when I am old and gray, do not

forsake me, O God. Keep me alive until I declare Your power to the next generation, Your might to all who are to come"
(Psalm 71:17,18).

"...that you may tell it to the next generation, for such is God, our God forever and ever, He will guide us until death" (Psalm 48:13).

"...[Things] which we have heard and known, and our fathers have told us. We will not conceal them from our children, but tell to the generation to come the praises of the Lord, and His strength and His wondrous works that He has done. So that the generation to come might know, even the children yet to be born, that they may arise and tell them to their children, that they should put their confidence in God, and not forget the works of God" (Psalm 78:3-7).

As a Christian, you could let the following verse from Psalm 102:18 serve as your statement for writing. "Let this be recorded for the generation yet unborn, a people yet to be created [so that they] may praise the Lord."

It is more difficult for some people than for others to speak of their faith to family members. Some may be more comfortable with putting something on paper. Such words could be read by family members and others in years to come, even by another generation after you are no longer living.

The Apostle Paul traced the influence of generational faith on young pastor Timothy. His words inspire us with the value of passing on our faith. He wrote in 2 Timothy 1:5, "I have been reminded of your sincere faith which first lived in your grandmother Lois and in your mother Eunice and, I am persuaded, now lives in you also."

Bridge building opportunity

People complain about generation gaps. We all understand such fractures in relationships, and you may be experiencing such breaches now with your children or grandchildren, if you are in mature years. Or with your parents and grandparents, if you are in your more youthful years. In either case, focus more constructively on building bridges rather than whining about the gaps and chasms.

Writing your life story by honestly expressing your feelings, your responses to events and situations during your growing years helps to build a bridge. Younger readers will realize that grandma or grandpa felt the same way they may feel when faced with similar problems or circumstances. Your story can link the generations and survive your lifetime.

I addressed this in the *Introduction* to my autobiography:

"I find it exciting that my children and grandchildren, whether they realize it or not, are who they are and who they will become, in part because of my parents and grandparents and the forefathers of my husband, all the way back to the beginning of time. How awesome! Through my story I hope they discover some things to inspire them, as I have, through exploring our roots.

The above realization has motivated me to dig, while I can, for the treasure of our past so my children and grandchildren will be able to pass on that wealth of knowledge to their future generations.

Two of my granddaughters, Kelly and Kara, sent me the following words on a Mother's Day card when they were pre-teens. That gave me further incentive to live up to the expectations of those who come after me.

Grandma, you have a way about you that I someday hope to have.

You seem to have found the answers to so many questions that life brings.

You accept life for what it is, and you accept me for who I am.

From you I learn what wisdom really is.

You give me a sense of family, not just my immediate family but the family I never met.

Your firsthand accounts of how life was for you growing up are things I could never get anywhere else.

Grandma, you've added so much to my life... and you give me so many reasons to love you."

Legacy

I anticipate leaving Planet Earth someday.
Sooner or later this body of clay
will pass away, but that's OK
because I'll be happily Elsewhere
and won't need it anyway.

But I have a longing to leave
something of worth behind
something the next generation will find
of value, some kind
of stepping stones on life's road
to help steady their uncertain feet
as they walk in uncharted ways
and carry heavy loads.

I can bequeath no greater assets
when I leave this transient life
than the legacy of spiritual wealth
which I've received from The King.
And wonder of wonders—
each one of my heirs may claim
the whole estate, and inherit EVERYTHING![1]

3
Generous Benefits
Surprise Bonuses

I hope you are convinced of the importance of leaving a lasting legacy. You may be the only one who can fill the continuity gap in your family, who could record things that would be forever lost to the generations in your family tree who are still unborn. If you are a chronologically mature person, you may suddenly find yourself the matriarch or patriarch of your entire family. That is the role in which I find myself. I have already outlived all the people in my immediate family tree. I know certain things no one else knows, and if *I* don't record them for our posterity, no one will.

Dwight D. Eisenhower put it this way: "The past sharpens perspective, warns of pitfalls, and helps to point the way." One book on heritage writing suggested the following reasons to search your past: (1) to help you strengthen your roots by understanding and passing on the good aspects of the heritage you were given; (2) to let you break the cycle of the hurtful and negative things by leaving them behind; and (3) to assist you in charting a new course as you build a positive heritage for yourself and those you love. If the legacy package passed to you is not so admirable, you have the opportunity to start a new inheritance of love and possibilities.

Heritage writing in perspective

I know people who really say they don't see the value of writing their life story, who say they never will do so, not even record a scanty outline of people and dates for their descendants. That is their choice and no one is forcing them. I am sorry, however, that they are denying their posterity of the rich inheritance they could have left them.

I am writing this for those who sincerely feel that they have something of worth to share with others through their life and are willing to put forth the little effort it takes. The benefits are so great! Knowing one's heritage shows us that humankind has always faced difficult odds, and so have you, but the way ahead is surer and clearer if we look at what has been and take courage for what might be.

To live without a knowledge of one's heritage is to live without moorings, to be lost in the melting pot of society. If we deliberately withhold that from our posterity, we fail to provide them with a generational anchor.

In considering your past, you should avoid either being chained to the past or glorifying it beyond what it was. Simply stick to the facts. You are not writing fiction, nor are you writing a history book, although your story may include some historical material. It is worthwhile to search for your heritage because you make a healthy connection to your origins and link your descendants with it. A person with a sense of the past is one with a sense of destiny. You come to realize that you are a part of the continuity of life because none of us can claim to be self-made.

Of course you are qualified

You may be persuaded that passing on your life story is of importance, but you hold back thinking "I'm not a writer. How could I ever write my story? I would like to, but I'm not qualified." Correction: You *are* qualified. You *are* a writer. You probably write letters, notes to people, and keep records of one sort or another. Some have written in a journal or diary at times during their lives and put their thoughts on paper privately. Others are reluctant to expose their feelings even to a piece of paper. It is never too late to learn.

No writing experience is necessary. You don't have to sign up for a writing course or attend a writing conference. Books are available to help you with all kinds of questions to start your juices flowing. I listed some of those books for you, but I devoted one of my later chapters to interviewing yourself. That may be all you will need. You can do it!

Don't say that there is nothing interesting in your life or that nothing ever happened to you. Just start to write and see what you discover. All of us have been living through the most eventful and progressive periods of our history, and we have been eye witnesses. Connect those events with where you were and what you were doing and how you felt at the time.

Don't think of writing your life as such a huge project. Relax. You may want to write your story only for your immediate family. That is a noble purpose, and I applaud you for understanding the limits of your readership. Go full speed ahead. It will be worth it. It is possible your story may interest a wider readership, but don't think about that in the beginning. Concentrate on getting the raw material on paper in a rough draft.

The age factor

"*But I'm too old* to start writing my story." Ah, you are just at the ripeness of maturity to do a good job. You may be retired and have more available time now. You have a seasoned perspective on life and on yourself.

The sons of a retiree father in Iowa bought him a computer for his 86th birthday. He never learned to type so he used the one finger, hunt-and-peck system. Daily for two months their dad wrote and wrote and wrote about his past. Stories about people he had known and things he did flowed through that one finger. He filled several disks with the output of his phenomenal memory and his long-dormant creative talent.

His sons realized he documented some priceless family history they might otherwise never have known. Their father gave them a closeup of the 1920s and '30s with local color of the town where they were born and raised. The sons took on the editing job and had the 143 page book locally printed. They share with a wider readership a precious slice of life in past decades full of hilarious comedies and poignant dramas in the history of the heartland that only Bob Ecker could write because he was a principal player. You are never too old to write your life story.

"But I'm too young. I haven't lived long enough. I haven't finished living." You don't have to be finished with life to write things going on right now or that went on in your growing years. Those events and your response to them are fresh in your mind. Because you are part of the computer age, you have no excuse not to journal the happenings of your life now and continuing to do so as you keep living. Moreover, you are generationally closer to your root systems so you might know people still living who could tell you about your ancestry. Hurry! Ask them. Preserve your heritage while you can.

A young friend wrote his memoir about being a "military brat" and living with his family on army bases in many parts of the world. Another student, barely out of her teens, wrote of her experience and strong reactions against being sent off to boarding school in another country by her missionary parents who served in primitive areas of Africa. Still another wrote of her displacement from a peaceful rural area in the heartland to the heart of New York City. She described the traumatic peer pressure of an urban high school. You are never too young to start writing your life story.

"What if" scenarios

Let us deal with some potential "what ifs." What if you don't have a beautiful bundle of memories in your life that you want to write about? You don't want to hang out your tacky laundry on the line for all the neighbors to see.

Perhaps you have a substandard heritage that you would just as soon forget and not pass on to your family or to anyone else. The closet of your immediate past or your more distant past may be full of skeletons and scoundrels. You are not inclined to drag out your past. Since you have kept the door shut so far, why would you want to open it and let everyone else in?

What if you feel personally broken or fragmented? You are not sure what meaning, if any, your life has had. Why would you want to expose all those shattered pieces to your family? You have always been a private person.

Suppose you are adopted and have no knowledge of your blood heritage?

What if you are single, never been married and don't have children and grandchildren to whom you would pass on your story? Suppose you are married but childless?

None of those "what ifs" are valid reasons to keep

you from writing your life story. There is valuable therapy in doing so, far less costly than years of going to a psychiatrist. The most valuable benefit is for yourself. As you walk back through your life, encounter your past, face your fears, wrestle with your disappointments, collect your broken pieces, perhaps confront your failures, you can learn from them. This is your opportunity to forgive the people who hurt you or let you down, betrayed you or abused you. Such a walk back through your life carries with it the need for you to *forgive yourself.* Writing your life can be the healthiest exercise you can engage in.

    Here is an idea. If you have lived a difficult or troubled life, write your life anyway. Put it down warts and all, let it all hang out *and never show it to anyone.* That is your privilege. Simply by writing it, you may have accomplished your purpose. I think you can do more than that, but it is your call.

    When you face your past, it will not be able to hurt you again. You can work through the painful or difficult things with your perspective of today. Don't dig things up to have a pity party. Look the negatives squarely in the face, write how you felt at the time and what you learned. As you walk through your life again in its retelling, you see yourself in a new light. You can deal with negative experiences. We all have some or many.

    With God's help you can neutralize their pain. You can free yourself from the chains of what happened in the past by deliberately forgiving everyone including yourself. You don't want to get a hangover from writing your life story. Be careful to leave the past in the past when you finish, then move on. It is never too late.

You have no one close to whom to pass on your story or heritage? If you don't have children, consider nieces and nephews or other relatives. Some of their heritage may be the same as yours. Perhaps you have friends with whom to share it. If you are in your mature years, join a group where people gather to write and share stories of their lives. Be confident that you have something to say and someone wants to hear it.

You have no one at all? Consider writing your story to God. Dedicate it to Him. Walk through your life and become aware of His hand on you and His presence with you both in the negative and positive, joyful and painful events of your life. Surely there were some of each. God gave you life, you lived it for better or worse, and you survived to the present.

You are adopted and for all intents and purposes rootless? You are not rootless. Your roots run as deep as anyone else's, but you simply don't know what they are. Because you are the product of some heritage, your life still has great value. But you can skip heritage writing and plant *your new roots* by writing your own life story from the time of your earliest recall. You have a past, it is the one you lived during *your* lifetime. By starting a whole new root system, what you have to say is precious and worthwhile!

It is not selfish to recognize that *you* will be the one who gains the most from the effort of writing your life. I believe you will know yourself better. You will have a sweep of the history of your life that you could obtain in no other way. You have the opportunity to "have your life flash before you" in a deliberate, controlled way, not as they say it does when you face a death experience. By writing your story, you can *live your life over and still be alive!* You will see your life's pattern, and in the process you may discover things you didn't know about yourself. I know I did.

In all the above scenarios, you have still learned something valuable from living, even or especially from the darker events of your life. Put your acquired wisdom down. It is a priceless commodity.

We have it easy

A book on writing memoirs told about a pioneer woman crossing the country in a covered wagon who journaled her story each night by candle light. For ink she squeezed juice from wild berries during the day. You have it easy, don't you think so? In the past century when paper was more costly and scarce, some people wrote in horizontal lines on every available space on a piece of paper and then turned it sideways and wrote across the lines on the same piece of paper. It was tricky to decipher, but they were intent on writing their experiences. You are not living way back when people had to write on papyrus scrolls or chisel their stories in rocks or on the walls of caves. Do you still have an excuse? You don't have to own a computer/word processor or even a typewriter. Tablet paper is cheap and so are ball point pens by the dozen.

Exploring your motives

To help you sort out your motives for starting on your memoir, I will share how I felt about such an important venture. The following is from the *Preface* of my book *Czeching My Roots*.

"Why does anyone write an autobiography? Why have I dared to do so? Is it because I think I am *somebody?* Not in a proud or conceited sense, but *I am somebody* and so is my reader. Each of us is somebody special and important to God and to our family and friends. Because God invested life in me, He expects me to be a good steward by passing on to others the valuable things I learned. By writing my life story, I am creating an extension of myself that I hope has some permanency.

Speaking of the death of her maternal grandmother, Paula D'Arcy wrote in her book, *The Red Bird,* "I was stunned that [the family] barely knew her, although she visited us often. We knew names, dates and places, but we didn't *know her*. She hadn't let us in." Paula said she was sad because no one would ever be aware of her grandmother's true feelings, needs and loves. She lived and died and was never deeply known. They never benefited from her accumulated wisdom.

I definitely don't want that said about me. In this book I take you with me on the journey of my life and times and the generations before my life began. I haven't white-washed my failures or down-played my triumphs because it was God who led me all the way. I tried to be honest. I take responsibility for my failures. The triumphs or successes are because of God's grace.

I want you to know the real me, imperfect and vulnerable as I am. I want you to understand my dreams, hopes, feelings, needs, loves and hurts. I want to share my acquired wisdom. When you finish reading, you will know me even if we have never met. Those who do know me may discover some surprising things."

Fringe benefits

Be alert for wonderful fringe benefits of reaching into your past, especially into your childhood and growing years. I spent many hours searching on the Internet and inquiring among my hometown friends and was rewarded by finding 14 of the "old kids on the block" where I grew up. I reached back about 65 years for some of those "missing persons!" That search spread to their siblings. We connected through correspondence and in print with my autobiography since they shared many of my childhood and hometown experiences.

It took a lot of work, but a second bonus was to locate and meet personally a number of my first cousins with whom I had no contact while growing up because they lived in other parts of the country and because, for whatever reason, our families were not closely bonded. Some of them, now well into their seventies and eighties, I met for the first time. Their ancestral roots were partially intertwined with mine. Almost none of them had any information about our common roots and were eager for my researched and written record.

That bonus was compounded by making contact with their children and grandchildren who were still linked in a close blood line, although it was thinned out through marriage, as is our family line. A memorable line by Ma in *Grapes of Wrath* underscores the need for staying connected with one's roots. "How will our children know who they are if they don't know where they came from?"

As if that weren't enough happy bonuses, to pursue my ancestral research I traveled repeatedly to Czechoslovakia and found blood relatives, some of whom were my peers in age and relationship, and their children and grandchildren. I would never have known about any of them or been able to bond so warmly had I not gone on a search for my heritage. None of them knew I existed either. That, in turn, led to some of them visiting this country and meeting their blood relatives in America for the first time.

Hold on—almost all of the above discoveries turned up in echo form when I wrote my husband's autobiography in which I researched his family and heritage. I was able to find and establish ongoing relationships with many family members of *his* first, second and third generations on four continents. What a rich experience!

I can't even imagine what exciting fringe benefits and bonuses are waiting for *you* to discover in the process of writing your life story and researching your heritage. Tell me about it when you finish! ✐

4
Shorties of Significance
Characteristics of Memoirs

How many times have you heard someone say (perhaps you have said it yourself) "I've always wanted to write my life story but it seems like such an overwhelming task"?

Remember the question, "How can you eat an elephant?" The answer is, *"One bite at a time."* Don't look at the whole of it but only as one small step at a time. Look at it like laying one brick in the construction of a building and then another and another. Write in small portions, one memory at a time.

Memoir writing is made up of episodes, specific recollections of assorted memories. Each is a slice of your life that, in a sense, may stand on its own as a little short story. It doesn't need to have a plot, however. These episodes do not need to be earth-shaking events, nevertheless they are important to you. They may seem insignificant to someone else, but remember that nothing in your life is unimportant, if you went through it. Some call these little shorties *vignettes*, brief literary sketches, small word paintings. Pack your writing with all the details you can recall because they will give your readers the flavor and feeling that they are there with you, feeling what you feel, seeing, smelling, hearing and touching what you are experiencing.

Your memoir should be a leisurely story, informal and fun for you to write. Please don't think of it as a tedious research project. You should have the time of your life walking back through your time tunnel. It is also a walk into the innermost part of your soul. Such writing gives you an opportunity to listen within yourself and gain a perspective on your life. What has your life meant? Have you gained a sense of your personal identity? You probably have a certain perception of yourself which may or may not be accurate. As you write, explore that perception, examine and test it. You might be surprised what you come up with.

Painting images

People today are accustomed to visual images on TV and in the movies. They don't use their imaginations as much as in years past. If you want your readers to see and feel and experience your life with you, paint pictures with your words. Each episode you write about should be like a short canvas on which you will paint with as vivid colors as you can.

Using *metaphors* and *similes* is one way to paint with words. A metaphor compares another object or concept by saying it *is* another object or concept—which it literally is not. A simile is a figure of speech that compares two unlike things by pointing out a likeness. One thing is *like* another thing. "Memoir writing is *like* constructing a building." (That is a simile.) "Your writing will be a treasure to your family." (That is a metaphor.) I began with comparing my search and research to digging. Not the digging of a meaningless hole but the digging of gold from a mountain of past memories. (That was a metaphor.) I put it this way in the *Introduction* to my book:

"In all this digging, I have at times been fascinated, sometimes surprised, startled—also dismayed and disappointed—to find out some things about myself. I gained insights into some reasons why I am like I am. In part, it is because of whose genes I have. It is also because of early experiences and influences I still carry within my mind, body and spirit, all of which I pass on to my children and grandchildren.

I tried to work some magic by going back in a "time capsule" to my childhood and beyond that as far back as I could to introduce the people who are part of the genetic and cultural background of my children and grandchildren."

Another metaphor I used was that of an artist, whom I depicted as God, and myself as a canvas on which

He was painting my life story. I compared my life to a jigsaw puzzle in another chapter. And to God as the Potter and myself as the clay in His hands. I was like a detective following clues. A genealogy is like a skeleton compared to a memoir. I scattered those figures of speech throughout my story. You can create your own way of describing things in your life by using comparisons.

Spotlighting approaches

You can approach your bite-size episodes in various ways. The events of your life can be amusing, unusual, or very common and seemingly ordinary. They may have caused you to feel uncomfortable, happy, painful or frightened. Some of the situations may have been ridiculous, poignant or embarrassing. Perhaps traumatic and impacting you for the rest of your life.

As you walk through your personal memory lane, you will discover all sorts of emotional experiences, high and low, sad and joyful, to record. Focus your spotlight on them. They are all part of what you have become and are therefore worthy of putting down on paper as part of your heritage. Don't ever say, "I shouldn't have felt like that." You did and it is OK. Your memoirs are pictures of your life and times and that gives them merit.

Because this is your personal history, it is interesting to speculate where the word "history" might have originated. The Latin word *historia* leads us to see the word "story" in it. In the Middle Ages in Europe the term "story" began to be applied to the different levels or floors of certain buildings. The outside wall of each level had either paintings or carvings or sculptures depicting some historical event, often a biblical event. Each level therefore had a "story" illustrated on it. Thus began the reference to how many "stories" a particular building had. I saw some of those splendid, carved facades on buildings in Europe, especially on my trips to the Czech Republic. Certain cities are famous for that kind of historic architecture that attracts tourists from far and wide.

Collecting the slices into a pie

Your memoir is a collection of stories, of small paintings that make up the structure of your life story. It is up to you to weave together those written snapshots of your life with some theme. You may not know that theme until you are nearly finished and gradually notice a pattern emerging. Or you may be lucky enough to sense a theme or a pattern to your life before you begin. A memoir does not necessarily have a theme, but it is exciting to the writer and to readers when one unfolds. I hope you will learn something important about yourself that will give you a new understanding.

In my autobiography, looking back on my life from the perspective of more than seven decades, I realized that I spent a major portion of my lifetime rejecting my ethnic heritage as a Czech. I searched for the reasons why I wanted to get as far away from my heritage as possible, although I had a loving and supportive family and an outwardly happy childhood. Therefore I perceived one of my themes as *"The story of a Czech girl who didn't want to be Czech"* and followed through with that thread to sew my life story together. I let my readers know that theme from the beginning, so I quote from my *Introduction* again:

"When I look in the mirror, I can't change the fact that I am a full-blooded Czech. I have Czech body structure, features and characteristics. I have a confession to make, so I will get it over with, although I will go into further detail in the chapters that follow.

In my childhood and youth, I rebelled against my ethnic background. I wanted to hide my roots so deep that no one would see them. At that time of my life I disliked being part of a minority cultural group. Sometimes unkind people would refer to Czechs in a derogatory way. Such experiences contributed to making me shy.

I desperately wanted to blend in with my schoolmates who, in my eyes, didn't seem as outstandingly different as I perceived myself to be. In reality, they were also products of a melting pot society. I know now that my perceptions were warped. I even refused to speak the Czech language when I reached late childhood and teens. I was embarrassed in front of my friends when my dad spoke English with a heavy Czech accent and my live-in grandmother spoke no English. I was ashamed of my ancestry, although I knew almost nothing about the wonderful heritage and culture I discovered years later and of which *I am now justifiably proud!*"

If you establish a theme, be sure to carry it through and choose memories that contribute to it. It is satisfying to the reader if you come back and pick up that theme near the end of your book. You may have sub-themes which run along with your main theme just as a novel has one major plot and a number of sub-plots. Some of these will become obvious to you as you continue writing.

Turning points

Another way to weave your life story together is to trace and record turning points and bends in the road that changed, shaped and impacted your life. Most of us can recall such crossroads where we could have gone one way or another. The choices we made without a doubt determined the direction of our lives. I incorporated those thoughts in my final two chapters titled "View from the Summit" and "Living on the Summit." (I refer to my chronological summit.)

A book that proved helpful to me during the writing of my autobiography is Dr. Phillip C. McGraw's best seller, *Self Matters*. He offered some suggestions for self-understanding that coincided with the self-evaluation questions which I asked myself as I kicked off those concluding chapters. He urged readers to list the *ten defining moments*, the *seven critical choices* and the *five pivotal people* in their lives. That is an excellent exercise in trying to perceive what defines you. In short, what and who made you the person you are?

That is what I attempted to do as I wrote my autobiography, one of the most rewarding, creative, meaningful "workouts" (I use the word deliberately) of my life. I am the one who benefited most from tracing God's hand on my life and on my heritage before I was born. The insights I gained continue to give me perspective on what lies ahead. I adapted some of McGraw's framework into my own life summary but lumped all three of his categories into *"Defining Choices/Events/Learnings"* and ignored how many there turned out to be. The choices I made and their consequences really described all the chapters of my autobiography and contributed to the theme of my writing.

Pivotal people

An interesting and important way to knit your life story together is to recognize and identify the pivotal people in your life. Pivotal means of critical importance. They may have had either a positive or a negative impact on your life. I identified my pivotal person from the beginning because she was the defining influence on me from my birth to the time of her death which occurred when I was a young teen. I dedicated my autobiography to her. She died 62 years ago but her positive influence on me has spanned my lifetime.

She was my paternal grandmother, Frantiska Plachy Sprinclova whom I loved with all my heart and fondly called "Baba," an abbreviation of "Babicka," the Czech word for grandmother. After emigrating from Europe in her fifties, she lived with our family in Iowa and was my primary care giver because both of my parents worked.

Even during the latter years of her life and for my next 50 years, however, I rejected and distanced myself from my Czech ancestry. I spent a lifetime living in China and Asia in mission work with my husband. China was as far away as I could get. I never gave a thought to my own ethnic heritage during that time. For all practical purposes, I adopted my husband's culture, language and identity. Not until 1990 did I begin the serious search for my ethnic roots, 50 years after Baba's death.

In the process of trying to unearth the factors that motivated and molded the lives of my grandparents' generation and our previous generations in Europe, particularly of my grandmother Frantiska, I discovered the unique "hidden treasure" of her rich religious heritage. That led me to research it as far back as the 1300s and drew me to take several exciting trips to my grandparents' homeland for firsthand study. As I followed that ancient trail and the historic personages who were involved in that religious heritage, major unexpected chapters of my autobiography took shape.

Start thinking about your pivotal people and your defining events. I believe that will lead you to see some patterns in your life and make you eager to write episodes that will share them with your readers. ✎

My Puzzle

My life is a jigsaw puzzle and I don't know
what the finished picture is like
because the pieces don't come packaged
and sealed in a cardboard box
with the picture on the cover.

I foolishly try to force
the many look-alike pieces
into places where they don't fit.

The life puzzles of my friends
are not the same as mine
so they aren't much help.
It's awesome to think that God
made my puzzle unique
and it's never-ever been put together!

As each year passes, the pieces begin to fit
but not always. Why so many dark pieces?
I'd rather have bright and shiny ones.

Only God knows what my finished life puzzle
should look like. So I think I'd better
ask His help day-by-day to work my life puzzle
in His perfect way![1]

5
Memory Triggers
Interview Yourself

When I was a child on the farm, we had to pour at least a cup or two of water down the hand pump over the well to start the water flowing. Most of us need help to prime the pump of our memories. Perhaps you need some suggestions to start the water of your memories flowing freely.

Read for pleasure the autobiographies of others. Such books are great memory primers, and secondhand bookstores are an economical source. As you read, you may think, "Why, I had a similar experience, but I felt differently about it." Go ahead and write your own version in your memoir.

The most meaningful recollections you will write are likely the intimate details of how you felt in a certain situation, what the place looked like, how the situation or event affected your life or your relationships. For that kind of writing you need time. Don't rush. As you begin to "put on your thinking cap," as my first grade teacher used to say, you will begin to visualize a scene you are trying to recall. Suddenly you are there again and the words will come. You will be writing from "a stream of consciousness."

Memoir writing gives you a chance to introduce to your children and grandchildren some of the significant people in your life who may have lived before your children were born.

Interviewing yourself

One of the interesting and usually productive ways to jog your memory is to ask yourself questions. Many of us, however, don't know what questions to ask. This brief chapter may provide some sign posts to point you down the right path to your memory lane. Questions may be about your family, your ancestry, the house where you grew up, your neighborhood, school life, jobs or careers, romance, marriage, parenthood, and retirement. Other questions might be about the family you raised and the experiences of your children. But remember that a memoir is *your* story first of all, not primarily about your husband or wife or children or grandchildren. Focus on *yourself,* what you did, how you felt, how life affected you.

Entire books have been written containing almost nothing but helpful questions to get you started. I listed several of them in the *Resource* section at the back. Such questions invite you to select as you would from a menu. You wouldn't want to order everything on the menu in a restaurant, likewise, pursue only questions that are more relevant to your life.

Don't forget the obvious

You will want to put down more than bare facts but don't forget the facts, the obvious things like a location, a time frame, a name, or what relationship someone was to you. Dates and history links provide a background for what went on at different times of your life. Something so familiar and apparent to you like whether you are left or right-handed and what difficulties that presented to you may interest your family members.

Because my maternal grandmother died when I was very young, I wasn't sure whether she was born in Iowa or came as an immigrant child from Europe with her parents. I never asked my mother. I would like to have known what color her eyes and hair were because it might be a clue to why two of my granddaughters have bright red hair.

Other obvious things might be where you lived at different periods of your life, a description of your neighborhood as a child and what you did after school. One chapter in my book is titled *Neighborhoods as they were.* How did your parents and grandparents make a living? How old were they when they passed away, and what did they die from? That becomes important when hereditary tendencies are required for your medical records and those of your children. Did you have siblings? Did your family move a lot or did you grow up in one house in the same city and go straight through the school system in your hometown? Did you go to college, get a job right out of high school or go into the military? How old were you when you got married, or what were factors that caused you to decide marriage wasn't for you?

Memory sparkers that take more thought

I chose only a few sample questions to give you a springboard for your memory. Dive off into either shallow or deep water, as you wish.

What were your goals, dreams, and aspirations as a child, an adolescent, young adult, middle-aged person and now? How have your dreams come into conflict with reality? Did you abandon any and how do you feel about that?

Who and what have been the loves and hates of your life and why? Have the meanings of love changed for you over time?

When and where did you learn the facts of life? How have your ideas about being a man or being a woman changed?

What were your major stresses and how have you coped with them? Have you suffered an illness or accident that was a turning point in your life?

Was marriage something that changed your life drastically, negatively or positively?

How did you choose your major life work and has your choice satisfied you?

Have you overcome some handicap in life and how did you do that?

Have you been happy with the way you look? Have you been oversensitive about it, or has it been of little importance to you, including the way you dress? What is your present most comfortable outfit?

If you went to college, do you feel that you were the same person when you got out as when you entered as a freshman?

Is there any place you've been that you'd really like to visit again, or somewhere you still long to go?

And a few more...

Would you say you have been a go-getter or a procrastinator?

How do you handle being deeply upset or angry or disappointed?

What are you like when you are ill? How do you cope with sickness?

What are your pet peeves? Are you easy or difficult to get along with?

Do there seem to be any dominant personality traits in your family? Have you noticed such things in yourself or your children?

What would you say has been your philosophy of life?

What is your favorite thing to do when you are alone? Does being alone give you satisfaction or do you avoid and dislike solitude and always seek company?

Do you have someone you confide in, do you make close friends easily, or keep troubles to yourself? Do people naturally come to you with their problems or do you avoid such encounters?

What was your favorite year? Favorite age? Favorite season of the year? Favorite time of each day?

Are you still trying to achieve some of your life goals? Adding any new ones?

Is there anything you would have done completely differently? Was there a turn in the road you think you should have taken? If you could change anything in your life right now, what would it be? Do you have a character trait you'd like to change even now?

Was there something that you really did not want to do but had to do anyway? How did it turn out for you?

Have you ever witnessed something you can't forget?

Were you happier and more fulfilled at one period of your life than another?

Were you sad when school days were over or were you eager to leave it all behind?

What are you most proud of about yourself?

If you hold a fundamental truth about life, what is it?

If you had all the time in the world, what would you do? What haven't you had enough of in your life: Time? Money? Love? Freedom? Close friends? Success?

Bring your story to the present

Your family and your readers will want to know you *now*. If you are in your mature years, what you were becoming, you have become. How do you feel about your life and yourself at this moment?

One book suggested that you take a realistic look at yourself at the present time and describe yourself and your attitudes in five statements. Not how you wish you were, but what you are, what you think and feel right now. I tried to do that and profited greatly through that exercise to understand myself better.

I had the most fun and yet the deepest introspective workout as I wrote my last two chapters. I looked in the time mirror and described myself, not physically but internally. I dealt with my responses to and struggles with the life package that was handed to me by heredity, circumstances, and ultimately by God. I reflected on my life attitudes, the wisdom I hope I have acquired, the conclusions to which I have come.

Those are definitely the kinds of things I want to pass on to my family and posterity. Unfortunately, they are not always things about which you can speak easily and freely to the people closest to you. *But you can write them*, and they will be there for the years to come.

I projected my anticipations into the future and how I view the days and years I might have left in my life. I described how I would like to live them, how I was trying to live them, without giving the impression that I have arrived at some perfect point. I excerpted some of my conclusions in my chapter *Wrapping it Up* in this book.

I encourage you to do something like that but in your own way. Describing your life at present might turn out to be the most memorable part of your life story for your family and readers.

6

Enhance Your Content
Select Significant Extras

The variety of contents in your memoir or autobiography will depend on what you want to emphasize in your life and pass on to your family. Some memorists are satisfied with written text only. Others want to preserve a largely pictorial record. Your decision will also depend on whether your contents will be typed, computer produced and then photocopied at an office supply store, or printed on a commercial press. You can go all the way from spending a lot of money to spending comparatively little. I will discuss packaging in a later chapter.

A word about photos

You may include photos if you are happy with the results in black and white reproduction on a high speed copier. Photos that are faded with time can lose a great deal of resolution in such a process. It will be costly if you want to duplicate photos in color and in quantity, but you may want to include one or two color photos or use one on your cover. Be sure everything in your memoir has a clear title or sub-title and every photo has a caption or identification and date, if that is available and appropriate. Don't forget to apply to all your contents those trusty helpers *who, where, what, when, why and how.*

How many photos to put in is up to you. Some memorists don't include any, others put in dozens as well as documents. Be careful about your original photos. Protect them from sunlight, heat, insects, water and excessive humidity. Avoid using rubber cement or white paste because they contain harmful solvents. It is safer to handle photo copies of rare photos rather than originals.

In your memoir you can bunch photos together in the center, put them in the back matter, or distribute them singly in appropriate chapters. In my book I scattered them singly or in twos near chapters with related material, but in some of my other books I gathered them all in the back matter.

Here's how I decided on which photos to use. After eliminating many potential photos, I spread out on the table the remaining several dozen that I didn't think I could do without. I wanted to use them all, but the cost would have been prohibitive since the printer charged per photo to turn them into half-tones for the printing process. Painfully I put aside all but 16 which were the most precious few. They included several of the oldest I could find of my ancestors, the house where I was born, the house where I spent the first 18 years of my life, my parents, and the little chalet in the woods where I now live. I decided on some of myself at different ages, our wedding, my grown sons, and one each of the homesteads of my grandparents in the Czech Republic. I reproduced a simple map of the location of the Czech Republic in relation to the surrounding countries in Europe.

I found a priceless photo of my grandmother Baba at about the age she came to this country before I was born. Unfortunately, in the photo she had two children seated on her lap, and one child's head interfered with making a portrait of her from the snapshot. Because the photo was so important to me, for an extra charge, the publisher's graphic artist eliminated the child's head, faded out the background, and put an attractive antique frame around it to feature on the page with my dedication.

Other enhancements to your story

You can slip in pages of poetry, your own or your favorites, (you need to obtain permission to quote the poems of others) family sayings, anecdotes or humor, old letters, recipes, family tree, maps, newspaper clippings, statistics, documents, special awards, sketches, chronology—anything you wish. Because I have written and published books of my poetry, I included a number of original poems inserted at appropriate places in several chapters.

A word about the use of dialogue. Of course you

weren't present for events which took place before your birth or in another country or during a past era of time. And your recollection of conversations in your childhood may be hazy. But it is all right to imagine plausible dialogue between people of the past. There are many legitimate fiction writing techniques you can freely use in a non-fiction work to give your writing immediacy and vividness. I imagined a number of conversations with my grandmother through my growing years.

I included some ethnic recipes but tied them to my family experiences. I described sauerkraut making by stomping barefooted in the cabbage tub, how my mother made homemade noodles, how we cousins watched wide-eyed as Grandpa made wine and beer in his basement, the Czech apple strudel process spread all over our dining room table, and cottage cheese making from scratch to finally hanging in a cheesecloth bag on our clothesline.

I dramatically retold some folk tales my grandmother related to me in words she would have used, although she spoke the Czech language. (If you use any words lifted from another language, be sure to put them between quotation marks and explain their meaning. I used some Czech words throughout my chapters and also gave their phonetic pronunciation to provide flavor.)

Lighten up your narrative with humor. I let my dad describe how he backed his Model-T Ford up hills to keep the level of gas flowing in the tank. I told how I tried, as a three year old, to remove my own teeth after watching Aunt Anna take out hers, and getting skinned knees and elbows jumping off the porch flapping my arms as I tried to fly like the birds. I described my sweltering hot summer job during college days bundled in winter coat and mittens in the freezer department of the meat packing plant turning carcasses of huge hogs over on the conveyer belt and singing at the top of my lungs (I was alone in the freezer) to relieve the monotony. I revealed the comical circumstances of the first time my husband and I met. I told about the candles in the candelabra melting and dropping off during our wedding ceremony in a packed church in pre-air-conditioning days. My guess is that you have plenty of your own humorous stories to sprinkle throughout your memoir.

Travel highlights

You may have traveled to other countries and had meaningful adventures, as I have. You can avoid sounding like a travelogue if you tie in your personal impressions, your unique responses to what you saw or experienced. You can link the history of a place with how it related to your ancestors in whose footsteps you were walking.

When my search at long last brought me for the first time to the little village where my dad and grandparents lived so long ago, I described my deep emotions. I told about finding grandmother Baba's church and sitting to pray in the very pews where she must have sat as a young girl and later as a young widow left with six children. I imagined her thoughts as she worshiped there for the last time after selling her little home and all her possessions to pull up ancient roots and sail to America.

I wrote, "Baba and her teenage son Charlie successfully escaped thieves who lurked in unlikely places waiting to mug people leaving the country. Robbers knew that such people usually hung all their money in a bag around their necks. If someone stole it, they would be destitute because they sold everything and would have no home to return to. After authorities confirmed Baba's tickets on the ship from Hamburg, Germany to New York, they gave her a large tag to pin to her clothing with a number, her name, the name of the ship and her destination."

After doing the research about early immigrant voyages from Europe to America and their common experiences going through Ellis Island upon their arrival, I wove in those facts as Baba and her son doubtless experienced them. That turned what might otherwise have been dry details and statistics about Ellis Island into a "you are there too" dramatic scene.

Dealing with statistics

Statistics can be meaningful if you link them to family experiences. I wrote, "In the early spring of 1907, approximately the time my dad came through Ellis Island at the age of 17, records show that he was one of 11,747 immigrants to be processed on a single day." And "When my maternal grandfather, Antonin, arrived in Cedar Rapids, Iowa, the population was slightly more than 3,000. By the time I was born, the population reached 50,000." And "The year before Mother was born, professional baseball began in her hometown. Coincidentally, later she married a baseball player. Electricity for power and light reached there a few years earlier so there were already 6,000 lights in the town—but none at their house." And "In 1900, people were excited about gasoline powered cars that would run at the breathtaking speed of *25 mph.* An old photo shows my mother with a veil over her hat tied with a ribbon under her chin because the car had no windshield to protect passengers against *that incredible speed.*"

Lists can be interesting if related to your personal experiences. I wrote "When I was six, Dad and mother gave me a little roll-top desk on which Dad placed my very own early model RKO radio. I usually got my way to eat dinner at my desk and listen to my favorite programs: The Singing Lady, Jimmie Allen, the Air Cadet, The Aldrich Family, and Jack Armstrong, the All-American boy. I begged mother to buy Ovaltine because I needed to send in the inner foil seal with 25 cents to get a decoder badge."

A word about titles

Give a lot of thought to your book title and the titles of your chapters. Your book title can be a provocative launching pad to describe your whole memoir. You may not decide on your title until you have finished your story. It is customary to have a "Working Title" which you may change when your final title comes to you. You may find that the title of one of your chapters can become a good title for your book. On the other hand, you may be certain of your title from the beginning, as I was. *Czeching*

My Roots seemed to be a natural and my family and friends caught its significance immediately with the play on words.

You may add a sub-title to your memoir which further describes your contents. Try to keep both your book title and sub-title short. If your memoir will be more informally packaged, the length won't matter. But if your book will be printed, the design of the cover usually lends itself better to a short title.

When you choose chapter titles, again you may begin with working titles that describe the subject matter or time period you will be covering. Each chapter should have a new subject. A good chapter title helps the reader anticipate interesting things to come. Begin each chapter with a good opening paragraph, develop the chapter content, then wind it up satisfactorily or perhaps whet the reader's appetite in a suspenseful way about more to come. Be as creative as you wish.

Front and back matter

You may or may not want to include an *Introduction*, a *Preface* and a *Dedication* in the front of your more informal book. At least an *Introduction* is helpful to the reader so he will understand from the beginning why you wrote it. You might want or need to explain your book title. Perhaps tell what time period you are covering and what you are not including. A *Foreword* to a book is usually written by someone other than the writer and does not have to be included in a memoir. If you have arranged your writing into chapters and have inserted other material, you will need to produce a *Table of Contents*. You won't be able to know the exact page numbers, however, until you have set up your writing in its final form.

In the back matter of my book, I reproduced a brief family tree, not a formal genealogical chart. On another page I compiled a *Chronology* of memorable dates and events in our immediate family during my lifetime and backtracked to the latter part of the previous century. I titled it *Family Events*. This can make a significant contribution to your memoir by helping the reader locate the time frame of the episodes you wrote about. Some memorists slip in historical or political facts in their *Chronology* to provide a background for their stories.

Since I engaged in a lot of research to be sure of the accuracy of my documentation, I included in the back matter several pages I called *Selected Bibliography of Resources* and another page of *Endnotes* where I kept track of quotations within my text for which I had to secure permission or document.

Dealing with skeletons

As you write your story, you are the only one to select what to put in. No one is strapping you to a polygraph machine, putting you under bright lights and asking you embarrassing questions. You don't have to put *everything* down in black and white. Decide what you want to include that is meaningful to you. When my mother hung out our family laundry on the clothesline to dry, she always hung "the unmentionables" on the inside lines so neighbors wouldn't see them. If you truly have unmentionables, and we all do, don't mention them. You can still be honest by being discriminating.

While writing my autobiography, I discovered some heritage skeletons that I never knew about. A suicide, a runaway, some illegitimate children, alcoholics, wayward family members, many divorces, infidelities, and a lot of other things—all in long past generations.

Some of those skeletons agreed to come out of the closet because they contributed to the honest story line or there was a point to be made or something to be learned. Other skeletons wanted to stay hidden. I didn't force them out. When you write your story, you should be careful that what you say will not hurt anyone still living. You don't have to please some editor or publisher. The beauty of writing memoirs is that you are the boss-writer and in full control of your project.

A few more suggestions

Select incidents from your life that had strong emotional overtones, crises and turning points, but don't overlook the little stories that provide human interest and flavor. I wrote about giving up ballroom dancing lessons because the fat lady teacher who taught by having us dance with her, badly needed under arm deodorant. I described the awful odor when my mother cooked a liver and cornmeal concoction every week for my dog Penny in the days before commercial dog food. I told about my fear during my first hair permanent when beauticians hooked you up with electric metal clamps with wires leading to a monster machine, and I dreaded ending up with frizzy or singed hair.

    Recognize that your memory may be faulty about certain experiences, so don't push yourself to retell things that may be a little vague to you now. Sometimes we deliberately block out details surrounding traumatic events. I admit I must have blocked out everything about my grandmother Baba's death and funeral, as close as she was to me, even living with us at the time. So I couldn't write about it. Write only what you remember well and stick to the facts.

My Scars

I bear scars to prove
that I have not always coped:
Emotional scars, when I've been
misunderstood, censured, criticized
slighted and offended, hurt and grieved
separated from ones I've loved.

Sometimes I've lost perspective
when encountering changes
and in resisting them, I received scars.
When I've shed assumptions
of early years or faced disappointments
that turned to doubts and fears
I received scars.

Scars come from trying to hide
injuries inside. I'm not proud of them
but they keep me aware
that I have not always coped.
Scars prevent me from judging others
who may not have it all together
either.[1]

7
Get Ready, Get Set, GO!
The Writing Process

It is not too important to think about sequence as you begin to write your story. Start anywhere in your life, not necessarily with your birth. Perhaps with some dramatic (to you) episode from which you may flash back to your chronological beginning, if you wish. Or start with your parents or grandparents. It is your decision.

There is no right or wrong way to write your life story. Follow your way, whatever seems comfortable. Flavor it according to your taste. Record it through your own eyes, not how other people might have perceived it, or how you wished it had been, but how it actually was.

You don't have to write every day. Use small bursts of time that become available. Also write in longer periods that you can schedule. Perhaps an evening a week or a weekend occasionally. Once your writing juices begin to flow, you may not be able to stop yourself. If you are on a roll, go with the flow and put whatever can wait on a back burner.

Recognize realistically that you can't and shouldn't include everything. If you have discovered a theme that begins to describe your life story, select events or feelings that contribute to that.

Be confident. Plunge ahead in writing about the living you have done. What's not to like? This is about you. It is your book. Go ahead and use "I" as often as you like. You are not on an ego trip but candidly describing life as it was, what you thought, what you did, how you felt, how life affected you.

Relax as you write. It may be intense emotionally to travel back in that time tunnel and to view yourself in an objective way rather than the subjective way you traveled through the first time, but easy does it. Take quiet, reflective times to think about what you are discovering. Don't be afraid of ghosts. Most of them vanish when you write about them. While you carry out daily routines, your thoughts may be running ahead to something you want to include. Scatter pads and pencils around the house and in your car to capture butterfly ideas. Look forward to your writing time.

Just get your thoughts down during the first draft. Forget grammar for the time being, if it slows you down. Don't polish as you go unless a better way of saying something suddenly comes roaring at you. Leave blanks to insert some details or statistics later. Don't get stuck wondering about them or feel under pressure to research them right away.

The beauty of using a computer/word processor is that you can edit with ease when you are finished. You can add things, move paragraphs around, and delete unnecessary material simply with the touch of the keys. But even if you write by hand on a yellow pad, use lots of space, lots of paper. Write large and perhaps on every other line so you can add material easily.

Syntax hints

Use the past tense unless you describe a situation where action is still going on and your characters are having a conversation, real or imagined.

Choose simple words and write in your own voice as you would speak. Don't try to be literary or write to impress readers with your vocabulary. Cut out unnecessary words. Tighten your sentences.

Use specific words. Rather than saying your family went on Sunday afternoon rides, say "Dad drove us proudly around in his shiny black 1929 Hupmobile." Rather than simply stating that it was hot, you might write that the sidewalk in front of your house was so hot you scorched your feet when you tried to go barefoot. Instead of saying your dad was tall, you might describe him as "well over six feet with muscles that bulged under his sweaty T-shirt when he came home from his construction job."

Wherever possible, write in the active voice rather than the passive voice. Instead of "Heavy cakes of ice were carried to houses where signs were left in windows," better might be "The ice man carried his dripping cakes of ice to homes where he saw delivery signs in the windows." Don't get "comma-tose." Use commas sparingly. Keep your sentences short and your action moving. Separate long sentences into two. Go easy on exclamation points. You won't need many if your words have strength.

Realistic writing

Don't write about yourself as if you were a plaster saint struggling to keep from falling off a pedestal—always perfect, never making mistakes, always right. Not only will your family and other readers have a hard time identifying with you, they probably will not believe you. By the episodes you choose to write about, show yourself vulnerable and admit your failures. But don't dwell on them. You can write how you felt about such things but avoid putting yourself down, beating yourself over the head, or apologizing excessively for your shortcomings. You can and should talk about your successes. You are not bragging. You are telling it like it was. All such things are part of the mosaic of your life and everyone else's.

Mention people by name when appropriate. When writing about non-family members, it may be safer to use only first names. Be honest about yourself but discreet when mentioning the failings of others. It is not dishonest to respectfully withhold some things that might reflect negatively on other people. You may take skeletons out of *your* closet, if it is tasteful and relevant to your life story, but don't drag reluctant skeletons out of the closets of other people who may be offended—or worse. They may sue you for slander.

You are not writing a "True Confessions" book. Ask yourself whether what you are telling about is fair to all concerned. Is it common or public knowledge? Is it necessary to your story line? Will it embarrass anyone still living or their families? Will it hurt anyone's feelings or expose their secrets? Some things are simply better left out.

Feelings and sensual writing

Writing about your feelings is as important as facts in your life story, perhaps even more important to your readers. You were angry? Embarrassed? Afraid? Betrayed? Violated? Head over heels in love? Jealous? Absolutely elated about receiving an honor or achieving some pinnacle of success? You should write about it.

Some of us were raised not to display our emotions, so it may be more difficult to reveal them in print. In the case of your life story, your readers want to know *the real you* not an artificial person. You are after a lively, warm, personal and family history that your children and grandchildren can relate to. Expressing your feelings accomplishes that.

Yes, you will recall sad times as you look back. You may have regrets, recall bends in the road where you wish you had gone in the other direction, but overall, you have survived. You had your share of joys as well as heartaches, didn't you? Don't back off from sharing them with your family and perhaps broader readers. Your life had value. You have lived!

Your story should contain elements of both show and tell. Let your episodes speak for themselves. Show your reader the situation, describe it, bring him into it so that he will understand how you felt and why. You don't always have to tell him. But go ahead and say that something embarrassed you, if it did.

Appeal to the reader's five senses. You want to take him back through your time tunnel with you. He needs to feel he is there, not just looking on from the outside.

I hope you got wet with us when I described the slap and spray of the rotating sprinkler in our backyard as I ran squealing through it with my little neighborhood pal, Dot.

Did you play with us after dark under the streetlight when we tried to squeeze in one more game of hopscotch before our mothers called us in? Did you join us as we ran around with jars capturing lightning bugs—and help us keep them away from the boys who loved to squish them on the sidewalk and leave a luminous streak? Did you taste my favorite comfort food for an upset tummy—toasted bread spread with butter, sprinkled with cinnamon and sugar, cut into pieces in a bowl over which Mother poured hot milk? (I still prepare milk toast when I'm ill!)

Did you hear the thunder of rain on the tin roof of the cabin at Sokol camp in summer? Could you feel the heat radiating from my blistering sunburn after swimming in the river in the blazing noonday sun?

Did you smell the heady fragrance of purple lilac

clusters as I walked alone the several miles home from a high school play late at night—unafraid? Or the smell of the hay and the warm body of our cow Bossy? Did you visualize me as a three year waiting with my little tin cup for grandma to fill it with warm milk "directly from the faucet"?

Did you hear the roar of the approaching cyclone as we scurried for protection to our dark and cobwebby storm cellar? Or the mournful wail of the freight train whistle late at night when my cousin Martha and I were sleeping in the scary attic at grandma's house? Did you duck under the covers with us at every creaking noise?

You get the idea. Go to it.

Your soap box or pulpit

Your life story *is* the place to freely express your convictions, dreams, ideals and goals. You can do so with warmth and depth and sincerity without preaching or moralizing. Write about your own experience. People can't argue with that or discount it. They may not agree with your experiences or your conclusions or your own feelings about them, but they are *yours* not theirs. You write about them because you had them and they were important to you. Your family and other readers are learning about *you* from your story, and no one will stand in judgment.

If religion or spiritual experience was not an important part of your life, either positively or negatively, you will not be writing about it. That's OK. Many excellent autobiographies and memoirs of good friends and my students made no reference to any religious convictions. If your faith was important to your life, however, as mine eventually was, you are free to write about it. Your life story would not make sense without it.

My Christian faith did not became real and meaningful to me until I nearly reached my teens. From that point on, it became a defining factor for the rest of my life. In retrospect, the prayers of my special live-in grandmother and her quiet life of devotion laid the foundation for my spiritual awakening. I described that process as a significant part of my life story. It set the course for my education, my career, marriage, family, and my entire philosophy and world view. I integrated my experience into various places of my life story.

Some memorists wait until the *Epilogue* at the end of their book to sum up their beliefs, lessons they learned throughout their lives, and other conclusions. You may want to do that as well as weave such attitudes and convictions into different chapters of your book.

Daisy petals: You have time...you don't have time....

Writing your life story is supposed to be a rather leisurely work that can, of course, be spread over several years, if you wish. You can update your autobiography as you go along, unless you publish it at some point of completion to your satisfaction. None of us may think we are done living yet, and we hope to add some future experiences to our life story. What you have written may not, of course, be your "last word." On the other hand, *it may be*. If we are already in our mature years, whatever span of time that includes, or if we are approaching AARP membership, time is *not* on our side. So I encourage you to get on with your writing. Write as much as you can, rough and incomplete as it still may be in process.

My girlhood friend Esther spent more than a decade working diligently on a complicated genealogy chart. She also collected boxes and scrapbooks of intriguing human interest information about her parents and grandparents and was almost ready to start fleshing out her story. She delayed writing about her own eventful life story—but she intended to. She died of a sudden heart attack. None of her siblings or grown children or grandchildren have been inclined to take up the task. All her research material may be gathering dust in some attic or basement or has been disposed of. *Is* time on our side?

Realistically, time is never on our side even in younger years. Life at best is short. Life is fragile and the world around us becomes more dangerous and insecure each day. None of us is guaranteed a long life. A much younger friend, who had just become serious about starting her memoir, suffered a stroke. Her memory is impaired along with her ability to write and communicate.

Putting it a rather frankly, "It is time *now* to *pass on* your heritage before you *pass out* or *pass on*." This is not a matter over which you should procrastinate. Because you have lived, your story is significant to someone or to many somebodies. I hope you will start. Get as far as you can, if not to the finish line. Every paragraph is worth it. I wish my grandparents and parents had left *even one page* of written heritage for me.

You may or may not want to set a deadline for completion of your memoir. If you plan to finish by a certain family reunion, special occasion, or a birthday milestone, you will want to shoot for a deadline.

Please consider—if *you* don't do it, who will? If you don't do it *now,* then when?

8
Dig for Gold
Search and Research

If you are going to include ancestry in your life story, you are fortunate if you have a lot of information. Your ground may be soft and fertile. But you may discover, as I did, that the ground is very hard and you will have to sweat as you dig for lost treasure. In either case, it is well worth digging, and digging means research. No easy alternative.

I'll share with you how and where I dug, and it may give you some ideas for researching your story. Late in life when I finally came to my senses and became serious about exploring my ethnic roots, I looked over what digging implements I might have at my disposal to write my life and my heritage.

The ground where I initially dug was my own memory where I discovered many things I thought I would never remember. But there they were, stored and still available in vivid detail in the hard disk of my mental computer! I had never consciously called up some of them on my memory display screen.

Next, I dug into musty family records, but to my disappointment, my cupboard was as bare as Old Mother Hubbard's. I didn't even have the birth certificates of my parents or grandparents. All I had was my father's baptismal certificate recorded in what was later called Czechoslovakia, but at the time of his birth was called Austria. It was written in Czech, which I couldn't read, and dated 1890. I felt like a detective following clues and this was my first. I found crumbly old photo albums, but unfortunately many gems in our family treasure chest were lost through the years because no one identified or dated the photos.

The importance of "visitations"

People often quote the saying, "You can't go back." In some sense, you can't. The past is past. As the Chinese proverb goes, "You can't step into the same river twice" because the waters of the river have flowed on. In another sense, if that river is still there, you can revisit it. If you can revisit the places of your childhood and growing years, do so. Try to meet some of the people who are still living and tap into your own memories and theirs. Your story will be more vivid and fleshed out with their input. It will greatly stimulate your memories and give you a high dose of nostalgia.

After I graduated from college, married, spent years in Asia and eventually settled on the East Coast, it was not possible for me to return very often to the Iowa town where I was born and lived until age 18. But after my husband's retirement and my unexpected intense desire to search for my ethnic roots, I made an almost annual pilgrimage to my hometown, "the place of my crime." That was where I committed the rejection of my ethnicity.

I had written and published many books, including a number of biographies, but I didn't consider writing *my* life story. Those "visitations" motivated me to start, and I began to seriously collect and write episodes of my life. Not until 12 years later, however, with about eight more published books between, did I publish my autobiography. I knew I had to do much more research before my story would be ripe and ready. Because I wanted to write a historically significant and accurate book, it took me until I was more than midway in my seventies.

By the time I tried to tap into the memory banks of relatives and friends in my hometown who might shed light on the generation of my grandparents, few such people were left. I regretted not starting much earlier while they were alive. During one of my visits, I discovered a nearly 90 year old neighbor of my grandparents in Europe. She helped interpret my dad's baptismal certificate, and we dug out a number of valuable clues. She also gave me the old house address and a description and map of the village of my paternal ancestors. Another elderly relative on my mother's side gave me the address of the family homestead in Europe as it was at the turn of the century. She cautioned me, "I have no idea if any relatives still live there." A whole new (and old) world opened to me. My hometown "visitations" were beginning to pay off! I was on my way.

Some people from your past may still be living, so don't let the opportunity slip through your fingers. Interview as many as you can. Ask them every question you can think of. Listen to them patiently. Express appreciation. Take notes or tape record, if it doesn't intimidate them or hinder their flow of memories. They may be able to point your shovel to dig in directions you never thought of.

Digging deeper

I dug into history sources and reference books to learn about the times and places and conditions in Czechoslovakia where my forefathers lived and loved and worked. I wanted to know what motivated them to leave centuries of ancestry behind and sail late in the 19th and early in the 20th century to transplant their family trees from the Old Country, as they called it, to the New World of America. The results of that digging made up a chapter in my book.

Because I didn't recall that my dad or grandparents talked about the details of their voyage or arrival in America, I wanted to thoroughly research the typical immigrant experience through Ellis Island in New York during the years they would have arrived. I already described how I plausibly imagined Baba's journey in what I knew was the accurate setting. That developed into another moving chapter of my story.

I imagined the experiences of the early immigrants of my family as they settled in a land so foreign to them. What was Iowa and its people like when my first Czech ancestor arrived in the 1880s when he was scarcely out of his teens? My research reached as far back as the days of the Indians. I told you how I linked the actual events relating to my family members to what was going on in my hometown at the time. That birthed another chapter.

What difficulties did those Czech immigrants confront when they attempted to find work in cornfield country without knowing English and many without job skills? Some, like most of my relatives, had only a few dollars in their pockets when they arrived. But this was their adopted land. No looking back, no going back. I did more research and another chapter unfolded.

Having come full circle from strongly rejecting my ethnic background to joyfully embracing it late in life, I saw my birthplace in a new light. Much of my family's and my own early Czech cultural experience now made sense and I began to value it. Better late than never! I researched the courageous and creative attempts of Czechs to perpetuate their (and my) proud heritage while assimilating into American culture. I described the customs they brought with them, many of which continue to this day. I linked most of them to experiences our family had. That developed into another unexpected chapter in my story.

I had to go there and do that

I reached the point where research from books was not enough. I wanted to see for myself some of the ancient castles and bridges, villages and landscapes on which my ancestors actually gazed. I wanted to pass on those first-hand experiences to my family and descendants because they are part of our common heritage.

My husband and I had the rare and wonderful privilege many times to walk the roads, see the historic and cultural sites and visit villages of *his* birthplace and childhood in China. We walked the Great Wall, strolled in Beijing's Forbidden City, and traveled deep into the interior of China. We were delighted to meet the present generation there and were deeply moved by those who survived political revolutions, persecutions and imprisonments to remain true to their Christian faith. *But I was now eager to see places and people of my own ethnic roots. I wanted equal opportunity!*

All I had were two probably outdated addresses in Czechoslovakia and no live contacts. I wrote a *"To whom it may concern: Hello, is anybody there?"* letter to the addresses in both little villages of my ancestors. I introduced myself and asked whether any blood relatives were still there. I wrote in English because I couldn't write in Czech. I waited and waited. Months went by, and I became discouraged thinking I reached a dead end.

At long last two letters arrived, one from each place, written in elementary English obviously with the use of a Czech and English dictionary. Good news and bad news. No living relatives remained in grandmother Baba's little village, but an elderly descendant of Baba's neighbor warmly welcomed my visit, offered hospitality and said she would show me everything I wanted to see. The village of my mother's family, on the other hand, was full of relatives bearing her maiden name, and they enthusiastically invited me to visit. They expressed one fear, however. No one but a teenage granddaughter knew any English! (She was just beginning to study English in school and was the one writing the letter on behalf of her grandparents.)

At last it was my turn! God surprised me with the fulfillment of that long overdue dream to visit my grandparents' homeland. My first trip to the Czech Republic was in 1991 with my husband the year before he died. I had a strange and wonderful sense of belonging while there. Surely my parents and grandparents would be surprised about my eager visits. I wanted to avoid superficial generalizations and limited first impressions, so I repeated my Czechoslovakia "visitations" three times.

The entire mystery of my forefathers on both sides of my family was not only being solved but was blossoming. I was flooded with firsthand information and the joy of establishing warm relationships with living generations of my relatives. I surprised myself and them by still being able to speak, at least in a rudimentary way, the language of my childhood which I rejected and refused to speak during my teen years and during the half century since.

In my father's tiny village I was able to trace his boyhood experiences, visit grandmother Baba's church, discover descendants of their neighbors, family roots and religious roots. I visited cemeteries in both places. "Underground" is a great place for research because the grave markers often yield bountiful information. More than facts, I was looking for stories and human interest, and I was excited about finding so much. I had moved from *no* information to *scant* information to *prolific* information! I faced the happy dilemma of having to sort out *too much* material! Several more exciting chapters shaped up.

Striking a mother lode

Occasionally when mining ore or precious metals, workers come upon a major, rich veinlike deposit set off from adjacent rock formations. Shouts go up because their hard work paid off. The strike yields abundant and valuable metal. I felt like shouting when I began to follow the trail of my *religious* heritage.

Here and there in my research and reinforced by my recollections I found clues to something in my root system that strongly influenced my ancestry, especially the faith of my devout grandmother Baba. I sensed that something significant in that religious history probably "trickled down" directly and indirectly to *my* life and faith. That led me to search for and study my historical religious roots which I followed backward for centuries.

I took several purposeful trips to Europe to explore the very places where historic personages like the 13th century martyr, Jan Hus, lived. I wanted to visit Bethlehem Chapel in Prague where he dared to preach in the language of the common Czech people rather than in traditional Latin of the Roman Church. My ancestors could have been in his congregation.

I discovered that part of my root canal in Europe was the Moravian church. I traced its involvement with Count Von Zinzendorf who offered refuge to persecuted Moravian Czechs on his estate in Herrnhut, Saxony, Germany. I wanted to go there and visit the actual location of the sweeping revival that took place on Sunday, August 13, 1727. That event catapulted the refugee Moravians to launch the earliest worldwide missionary thrust in the 1700s which predated the modern missionary movement. All that was the background for the Czech Evangelical Reformed Church in Europe that later spread its branches to America. That was the church of my forefathers.

Bringing it full circle

During the writing of my life story, I had the privilege of doing all the above and much more! I had rich experiences indeed, and I felt satisfied to have researched my roots full circle. Several chapters that I would never have dreamed possible to write took shape after I walked in the footsteps of those great men and women of faith and courage.

I linked this to my life story. Because of my intense study of those events, I discovered that in some quite marvelous and mysterious way the *"faith of my fathers living still, in spite of dungeon, fire and sword"* was *my* heritage and the heritage of my children and descendants.

I wrote how it is possible and plausible that the prayers of my distant Czech ancestors on behalf of the generations yet unborn, *which includes me*, had some predestined influence on my life. And that my lifetime of involvement in overseas missionary work was perhaps not only my decision, the call of God on my life, but in part the result of the prayers and background of my ancestors in past centuries. I would not have known any of this had I not become involved in writing my life story and reaching back in time for those underground roots.

Linking history to real life

When I wrote about my dad escaping from his homeland in Europe to avoid conscription into the army, I had to find out *what* war was going on, what army, and the whole context of the times in the Czech Lands. When I researched the Great Depression of the late '20s and early '30s, it was to understand its effect on *my* parents and their business ventures and my early years.

When I described my high school years, I set it in the context of World War II and how it affected *our* family—ration cards, rolling bandages, gasoline shortage, and knitting sweaters for our soldiers. I told what was going on in the whole world and then narrowed it down to my world as I watched some of my classmates skip graduation exercises and leave school early to enlist in the army. I described how I felt when I heard that some were killed in action. When I first heard about the Japanese attack on Pearl Harbor, I described it in the context of a quiet afternoon at a friend's home interrupted by her dad rushing in to shout the news.

To add human interest and tie in personal history during my high school years, I itemized "this was in the days before...." The list may be almost unbelievable to the younger members of my family and readers who wonder how we could have lived without all those things. *We didn't miss them because such things weren't even invented yet!*

Are you having fun yet?

A cliche, I know, but by this time *I was having a ball* doing research! Such digging doesn't need to be boring as you thrill with the adventure of walking through times past that impacted your forefathers. You will surely enjoy yourself on the particular "dance floor" of the years of your own life and experience the delight of "dancing with your ancestors" in the world in which they lived.

I shared with you at length the process of my research to inspire you to do yours. Who knows where *your* detective search for your roots will lead as you launch into the writing of *your* life story? Take the challenge. Go for it! ✏

Music Score

The last score of the song of my earthly life
will it be in a major key? A majestic symphony?
I'd like that, Lord!
To crescendo fortissimo, with a sustained
final note
followed by thunderous applause
maybe an encore or two, a standing ovation
to climax my life performance
with glorious elation!

But it just may be that You've chosen for me
a simple, closing melody in a minor key
not melancholy, but plaintive and gentle
generous with rests, closing pianissimo.

I cannot choose my life score.
Both lyrics and chords are selected in advance
by You, my Divine Conductor.
You have the floor. What's more—
I don't perform alone.
The orchestra has many players, not just me
whose melodies You bring in
to achieve Your perfect harmony.

But the finale is assured: The ovation is for YOU!
The "Hallelujah Chorus" echoes throughout
Your creation.
So I'll watch Your eye, heed Your hand
I'll play or be silent at Your command
and be content with the musical score
You've prepared for me from ages before.[1]

9
Wrap It Up
The Final Touch

An *Epilogue* simply means a concluding part. In a *Preface* or an *Introduction* you tell readers what you intend to say. In the body of your story you say it. In an *Epilogue* you summarize what you told them and what you want them to conclude from your story.

You may or may not want to write one. Not everyone does. But it is your opportunity to sum up your life, to philosophize. You can talk to your readers face to face, as it were. You can emphasize what you want them to remember about you. This is your platform or soapbox or pulpit so take full advantage of it. If you have not done so within your story, here is a place where you can also share your religious beliefs and how they affected your life.

In an *Epilogue* you can share your hopes and dreams for the future of your family and even unborn descendants. You can talk about your values, what you feel are the most important things in life and in *your* life.

You can give tribute where tribute is due. You can express appreciation and pride in your family, as you look forward and in your ancestors, as you look backward, if that is appropriate.

You can write a prayer for your descendants, if that is your desire. You can give a blessing by writing that blessing as you pass the torch to the next generations. Perhaps a poem, yours or someone else's, will express the concluding words you want to say.

Here you can be as sentimental as you wish. This is your turn at the microphone. Say all the important things you would say if you thought those words were your *last* ones. Be sure to finish on a high note, however.

I included a short *Epilogue* in my autobiography. Among other things I wrote:

"In an awesome and unique way, both Ted and I inherited a rich legacy brought from both the continents we represented. That bequest is incomparably more valuable than money or any buried treasure because it wasn't buried—it was freely shared.

The Christian heritage our grandparents left us, although they spoke different languages and lived far apart on this Planet, was no accident or coincidence. We believe it was appointed by God for His eternal, sovereign purposes. *That's* the legacy we want to leave."

I included a poem I wrote titled *Legacy.* I inserted

some of my original poems in several other chapters of my book where the topic fit my story. Ralph Waldo Emerson wrote, "Rings and jewels are not gifts, but apologies for gifts. The only gift is a portion of thyself." You may never realize how the gift of yourself in the writing of your life story will affect those who come after you, some of whom you will never meet.

Further on in my *Epilogue* I pointed out that the Christian faith to me was not a family tradition I was trying to pass on because it could not be passed on or inherited. It was a relationship with God and a matter of each person's inward and individual response. All I could do was point the way to the treasure of our faith and affirm that I have proved it true, that God is faithful through all difficulties and struggles. I continued with the hope that our descendants would receive that faith for themselves and experience *God's promised generational blessings and favor* upon our children and children's children.

To bring my story full circle I tied in the theme of my book with metaphors I used in the beginning of my story: digging for treasure, finally finding the treasure in the "faith of our fathers," the simile of our family tree, the branches and twigs, and concluding with "the trunk" comparison. My final paragraphs were:

"Our heritage roots were not in fertile ground from the beginning. Both sides of our family tree on two continents were planted in soil that was rough, stony and unfavorable, and family relationships were far from ideal. But

God stepped in and nourished both of our ancestries in that inhospitable ground with the warmth of His Son, the rain of His goodness and the nutrients of His mercy. It turned out that both Ted and I *did* grow up in the *good ground* of God's love and according to His predestined plan.

Our family tree became strong and fruitful under God's care but not without the painful and necessary furrows of God's cultivation and transplanting. God was there all the time tending its growth, pruning, nurturing and protecting it. He lovingly continues to care for and watch over our spreading family tree from the *trunk* upward and outward to the furthest *branches* and young twigs. *To Him be all the glory!*"

Within the early chapters of my book I already described my personal journey to embrace the Christian faith and establish a personal relationship with God. I followed the threads of that pivotal decision and commitment in the chapters that followed. I described my struggles as a sullen, unhappy child and early teen with a giant size inferiority complex, volatile temper, self-will, low self-esteem, and an unreasonable rebellion against my ethnic identity. I was a shy, only child under the care of my grandmother and felt neglected by my working parents.

Restless and dissatisfied with everything and everybody in my life and harboring a bad attitude, I nevertheless secretly sought for God in my inward heart. I described my path to faith, how God reached to me and I reached to God, and my later understanding of what part my heritage may have played. The eventual but gradual changes in my attitudes and life led me to the far corners of the world, to China.

I brought my reader with me as I waded through scientific and theological questions to form a philosophy of life or world view in college where my personal faith was tested. Telling my story honestly, I confessed taking some wrong turns on that faith journey and struggled with the results of misunderstanding my priorities in ministry. I described my dilemmas when confronting my mistakes. In other chapters I traced the way my faith in God brought me through life-threatening cancer surgery and through widowhood.

Therefore, I didn't need to pack all that into the *Epilogue*. My readers already walked through my faith experiences with me.

Chronicling your life lessons

I devoted the two final chapters of my autobiography to the actual wrap up of my entire life. In fact, I consider them as the most important chapters of my book. In them I did the reflecting and summarizing that is often done in an *Epilogue*. Typically, an *Epilogue* is rather short. I needed more elbow room for what I wanted to say in conclusion, so my last chapters are entirely devoted to those thoughts.

I titled the next to the last chapter *View from the Summit* and the last one *Living on the Summit.* I refer to my chronological summit. You may profit by knowing how I developed them. You may glean some ideas, but you can do as you like for your wrapping up. It is your story. I began the *View* chapter with:

"The top of a mountain should be the best place to see the entire 380 degree panorama of life. The look backward should be satisfying—not proud, not disappointing or full of regrets. The look around should be one of contentment and joy. The look ahead should be exhilarating with anticipation. *That is largely true of my life at this writing in the latter half of my seventh decade.*

Being at the *summit* also implies *summary*—what I learned from the long, steep climb. If I can't tell what I learned, 75 plus years were a wasted trip. But since the Lord has been my Master Teacher, through sunshine and shadows, I learned a lot.

A children's song goes something like this, if I remember correctly:

"The bear went over the mountain...(repeat) ...to see what he could see...(repeat)."

(Next verse) "The other side of the mountain...was all that he could see...." (repeat)

Early in life I decided I didn't want to be like that frustrated, disappointed bear who spent his time and energy on such a climb only to find nothing at the top or on the other side. I would try to evaluate my life as I went along to be sure I had the right goals in view and my ladder was leaning against the right house.

For years I've tried to live the examined life, which Plato said was the only life worth living. I didn't want to arrive at my chronological top of the mountain with a backpack full of regrets, nor view the other side of the mountain with disillusionment, despair or fear. At intervals, at least once a year, I try to take time out to ask myself specific, searching questions and write them in my journal. My answers aren't for anyone else but God to see. He is the Searcher of hearts.

I wish I had begun that self-evaluation practice earlier. Had I done so and continued it more regularly, I could have kept from taking some detours for which I do have regrets. However, I deliberately don't focus on those now. I confessed them to God, repented of them, turned from them and have the assurance that God has forgiven me. Both God and I remember them no more. I keep moving on."

I continued with life evaluation questions that reach into the depths of my inner person, to the core of my authentic self. Questions like knowing my purpose in life, goals, limitations, measuring success, self-worth, issues I am passionate about, and what I learned from the darkest periods of my life.

Zeroing in on questions relevant to my latter time of life, I speculated on how many physically, mentally and spiritually productive or alert years might realistically lie ahead for me. In view of that, on what priorities I should be focusing, and how I could limit or eliminate things that might be holding me back from completing what I perceive is God's continuing purpose for my life.

Going back to a beginning theme in my book, I asked myself whether I am satisfied with what I have become and with what God painted on the canvas of my life. In this chapter I came full circle with the similes I used throughout the book: God as the Master Artist, the Potter, and my life as the jigsaw puzzle in a box where I couldn't see the picture on the lid.

I put much thought in developing this chapter around my realization that all my defining moments and pivotal people have resulted *from my own choices*. The decisions I made and their consequences describe my entire life. As a stubborn, self-willed young person, I wanted to be the captain of my own ship, and I didn't want anyone to tell me what to do. I briefly focused on a number of critical choices I made in my life and where they led me. The most important one was to deliberately surrender my self-will to God's will and let Him steer my life ship. I explained the final one this way:

"Decision: A critical, defining choice I am making right now is to ignore the trivial limitations of aging and live fully each day of the rest of my life. I choose to live in anticipation that 'The best is yet to come!' *I look forward to living on the summit.*"

That transition phrase introduced my final chapter with that title. An excerpt from it follows:

"How then shall I live on my chronological summit for as long as God gives me life on Planet Earth?

The summit of a mountain usually isn't a plateau. I don't believe the summit of my life should be a place to settle or let down my guard. As I look around my mountain top, I see more peaks to climb. My life is not yet spent. I'm still spending it, even if I have only one day left.

If I don't keep growing, climbing, moving, I will slide backward. Doctors say that this applies to both the aging body and mind. 'You have to use it or you'll lose it.' If I don't keep my mind alert, it will deteriorate in the same way my body does. The latest medical research gives us some previously unknown and unexpected good news. Even in older age, the neurons (nerve cells) in the brain *can renew themselves* and new stem cells can *grow!* That's not news to God. He created us with that capacity and expects us to 'be transformed by the renewing of your mind' daily (Romans 12:2). Therefore, I want to push the horizons of my mind and spirit further and remain on the cutting edge of life. The more I stretch, the higher I can reach. I don't want to miss anything God sovereignly planned for me....

Summit time is my opportunity to thank God for blessings of the *past*, to celebrate the *present* and anticipate the *future*. The following is my philosophy of life at this chronological season. I shall 'put my house in order' not to *retire or expire* but to *refire*. I spelled it out for myself in these major areas:

> *Focus* on keeping the *main thing* the main thing.
> *Simplify* my material "stuff."
> *Prioritize* my goals and time and efforts as if I had *little time* left.
> *Anticipate* that God will still give me *generous time* to live for, serve and glorify Him.
> *Obey* fully and do promptly whatever God reveals as His will and purpose for me.
> Keep *sowing and reaping* at the same time.
> *Celebrate* each day as a gift from God.

That *main thing* that I want to keep in focus is to put God and His Kingdom first by coming into His presence and seeking His face each day...."

I spent the rest of that chapter developing those aspirations and applying them to my life at this final season. I sneaked in one more chapter only a page long titled *Unfinished Symphony*. I wrote:

"I can't write the last chapter(s) of my life because I haven't lived them yet!

I'm on tiptoe of anticipation to discover what gold God still has for me in my original treasure chest—how much I can keep learning, how close to God I can become and what fruit I can still bear for Him....

To add another metaphor, my life at this point is an 'Unfinished Symphony.'"

I concluded my autobiography with another original poem titled *Music Score,* which did wrap it all up.

How you wrap up your life story is entirely up to you. You may want to spend some quiet, reflective time considering that because it is so important. You may have a lot of living to do yet, many years ahead, but in a way, you can look at this writing as the sum of what you want your family and others to remember. It is the valuable legacy you want to leave behind, and you get to tell them while you still have your wits about you!

Your Invitation

If you really write your memoir after reading this book, let the author know. She will be delighted to congratulate you personally!
Write to: Leona Choy
Golden Morning Publishing
P.O. Box 2697 Winchester, VA 22604
or contact her at:
http://www.goldenmorning.com
or e-mail: leona@goldenmorning.com

10
To Market—To Market?
Polish and Package

Eventually you will reach a point when you are finished saying what you want to say. Don't stop *too soon* by getting bogged down with details and give up before you should. Don't go on *too long*. Your reader may be afraid you are trying to include everything you ever did in your entire life. A long life doesn't mean a lengthy book.

When you've reached your finish line, put your writing aside for awhile. Give it a rest. Let it cool. Then read it with detachment as if you were someone else or that person you visualized for whom you are writing. Now is the time to revise and polish.

Are you *really* done?

Double check names and dates and historical facts. Because you are so familiar with your story and have probably read your story so many times, your eyes tend to skip over errors, even obvious ones. If you have spell-check on your computer, it still may not alert you to mistakes if it comes to a word that is a valid word but not the one you intended. Examples are *there* and *their, due* and *do* and *dew*, *mail* and *male*. If you have some doubt about a proper word or the meaning of a word, be safe and check the dictionary.

Ask yourself whether everything you included contributes to your general theme.

Have you covered the points you said you would in your *Introduction?*

Do your chapter titles match what you wrote about?

Does the order of your chapters make sense? Are they chronologically progressive? Do you need any transition paragraphs to make a bridge from how you ended the previous chapter to how you began the new one?

Each paragraph should deal with one point. Do you need to make some paragraphs shorter because they contain too many ideas? Short paragraphs are easier for the reader. In today's writing even one or two sentences can be a paragraph, especially when you want to keep the action moving. The English language is constantly changing, so don't get hung up on too many grammar rules.

Watch for things you can leave out and for some gaps in your story that may confuse the reader.

Have you been honest about yourself? Have you written enough about the *interior you* to balance all the *exterior things* that happened to you? I began my chapter titled *A Glimpse of The Artist's Plan* with these paragraphs:

"I shared with the reader in previous chapters primarily the *outward* things that happened in my early life, my environment and some events influencing my impressionable childhood. Equally or more important was what was going on *inwardly*—my personal response to those outward factors. The outward was only an overlay of my inner person. Both aspects shaped my future.

I can't go further with my life story without revealing what influenced the direction of my life for the next three-quarters of a century. My decision would affect the lives of my *branches*—my children and my children's children, perhaps the lives of our future generations."

If your writing was a search for your own identity, have you found yourself? Do you understand yourself better for having walked through your life realistically?

Have you been fair to your family members as you portrayed them?

Read your manuscript aloud. That will often show up your overuse of certain words and sentences that may need to be divided.

Be sure you identified a person the first time you mentioned him or her. You don't have to keep identifying him in later chapters.

A few more check points

If you included dialogue, is every instance properly punctuated before and after?

Do your subjects and verbs agree?

Is your use of tense consistent?

Sentence fragments, if intentional, are acceptable in more informal writing and in dialogue. Have you varied the length of your sentences so they don't become monotonous?

The trend today is toward fewer punctuation marks. If a short sentence flows smoothly without a comma, eliminate it. When a slight pause is needed as you read a longer sentence, add one.

Did you use a fancy word where a plain one would do? Have you used too many words to say something simple?

Do you have enough dramatic scenes and dialogue to break up the monotony of the narrative?

Could you change still more verbs from the passive voice to active voice?

Have you written in your normal tone of voice?

If you wish, give your manuscript to one or more members of your family or a friend for an objective reading. Tell them specifically, however, what you want them to look for when they read. You are probably not asking them to critique or criticize or evaluate it. It is your story, your life, and you are going to say what you want to say.

Perhaps you will ask them to watch for spelling errors, wrong punctuation, grammar mistakes, repetitions, wordiness and lack of clarity. When your copies come back, thank your friends and make those corrections, *if* you think they are valid.

Packaging your story

How many people do you realistically think might want to either buy or receive copies of your life story? How much money do you want to spend to publish it? The answers to those questions will determine the kind of packaging you will use.

The simplest way to go if you need copies only for your immediate or extended family and a few friends, is to first type your pages neatly or have someone else do it. For a consistent printout it looks best if done on a computer with a word processing program. Your pages can be numbered automatically within the program, and you can select different fonts for your chapter titles and the book title. A caution: After you have turned it over to the typist, it is too late to revise it. You should have caught all your errors and corrected everything.

Before you take your typed pages to the office supply store for duplication, you need to decide whether you want text on both the front and back of each page or leave the reverse side blank. When pages are printed on a high speed copier, they will collate (assemble the pages in order) automatically. When you have reached that point, you will be able to calculate what your book will cost per copy, since the charge for duplicating depends on the number of pages. If you want both the front and back of each page printed, understand that the price is twice the cost of a single run.

If you have a short book, it can be stapled or put into a binder or folder. Inexpensive but attractive covers are available, as are transparent covers in clear or colors. If you have a larger volume of pages and plan to put them into a school-type three-ring notebook, office supply stores will tell you the cost for punching holes in each page. A three-post clasp binder is another option.

You may prefer spiral binding (called comb binding) which is available for an extra charge but still quite economical. With the title perhaps printed on colored cover stock, you have an attractive binding for your memoir and the pages turn and lay smoothly.

To sell or not to sell

Remember that you are the one who will have to distribute or sell your self-produced memoirs. Realistically, your family, relatives and friends will probably expect to receive complimentary copies of your book, and selling them will not be the way to go. More informally packaged memoirs are usually understood as being for private distribution since they are a limited edition. That means you will have to bear all the cost of production yourself unless some thoughtful and generous family members offer to help you with the costs.

Going the book route

You may decide to put your completed life story into actual book form because you anticipate a wider readership beyond your immediate family and friends and you have the funds to follow through with your dream. Some memoir writers are fortunate to turn over their completed manuscript to a son or daughter or other family member who will make all the decisions, pay the costs, and see the production through to completion. But I am addressing the memorist who is planning to see the process through by himself. Let us explore your options.

(1) Do you expect a commercial publisher, called a *royalty publisher*, to be interested in your book for sale through their catalog and bookstore outlets and marketed and promoted through their company? To be completely honest and realistic, such publishers are seldom interested in private memoirs unless written by a celebrity or someone of national importance or professionally expert in some specific field (politics, religion, education, etc.). The publisher wants to be sure a book would have a large readership so he would not only recoup his initial investment but make a sizeable profit. A publisher runs a for-profit business. He is thinking in terms of hundreds of thousands of copies being sold in a short period of time. He is not inclined even to consider what he calls "risk books" which may not turn a profit.

The reason a royalty publisher is so reluctant about accepting any manuscript for publication is because when his company offers a contract to an author, the publisher assumes full responsibility for editing, publishing, printing, and distributing the book. He then pays the author a stipulated royalty which is comparatively small, usually ten percent or less based either on the wholesale or retail price per copy actually sold.

Royalty publishers often assign their own staff either to write or edit or collaborate with an author on an autobiography *they* have asked for. Seldom if ever these days will a publisher even look at a book manuscript that he didn't ask to be sent to him. It is not unusual for a package containing an unsolicited manuscript not even to be opened. It may either be returned to the sender or, if return postage does not accompany the package, be put into the wastebasket.

In general, a royalty publisher will seldom consent to look at a finished manuscript. He insists on his editors being involved in the process of writing it. They know exactly what will sell and want the manuscript written according to their editorial specifications. The way an author starts the process is by sending a carefully crafted query letter accompanied by only two or three sample chapters, an outline and summary of the rest, and his credentials for writing. An author has to do a professional job of persuading the publisher even to take a look at his writing.

Enough with the cold water! What are your other options, if you want your memoir produced as a book?

(2) You could consider *private printing by a commercial printing press* perhaps in your hometown. You then become the publisher and bear all costs of cover

design, format, actual printing, advertising, shipping, (if the press is not local) and distributing. Photos and almost anything except straight text will cost extra. If you need a graphic designer for the cover, the expense is high. If you go to a job printer, be sure to get several estimates and calculate carefully how many copies you will need. You don't want to end up with cases of books piled in your garage which you can't sell. Copies you actually sell will help pay for your initial outlay, but copies you give away are exactly that, no profit. By going to a private printer you do have control over the whole process, but you must make your own decisions and do your own selling.

Don't go there...

(3) Next is an option I do not recommend, but which many inexperienced writers fall prey to. Beware of a deceivingly similar but vastly different publishing route. *Subsidy* publishers sometimes called *vanity* publishers actively solicit books by flattering the author. They are known for accepting any book manuscript whether or not it is saleable or is quality writing. They lead new writers to believe they have an outstanding book which will make them rich. A respected marketing book advises, "Avoid these. Nobody respects them. They prey on your general ignorance of publishing."

In subsidy publishing, the author pays the publisher to produce a book for him. Not only does the author finance the entire production, but the subsidy publisher profits on every book he produces. He customarily inflates the actual costs to assure himself of a profit on the initial production of the book. He may not really care, therefore, whether your book sells or not. You still have to do your own selling.

In the subsidy process, the author does not have control of the entire project and pays out more money to have the book printed than he would if he hired a commercial printer. In some vanity contracts the author doesn't even own the books he paid to be published. He receives a few free "author's copies" then is "given the privilege" of buying more copies (of his own book) at the "author's discount."

The review copies which the subsidy publisher may promise to send out, often go straight into the wastebasket. Periodicals or reviewers recognize the name of the subsidy publisher on the spine of the book and are reluctant to recommend it. You paint yourself into a corner by publishing with them. They are known for doing a "snow job" on the author by printing a few, attractive news releases which they may not even mail. Bookstores are rarely willing to accept vanity press books to retail. Libraries usually do not acquire them for their holdings.

Subsidy publishers are out to make a profit on the author and usually persuade you to order more copies than you need because they profit on each one. Please understand, what subsidy publishers do is *not illegal.* Business is business. If the author is aware of all arrangements and clearly understands and agrees with all the complicated, small print in the contract and doesn't care about the higher cost, he is certainly free to go this route. Most professional writers are against it, but any author has a right to do as he chooses.

Vanity publishers do promote their services widely in paid ads even in respected writers' magazines. Some of the names to watch out for are *Vantage Press, Inc., Dorrance Publishing Co., Carlton Press* and *Rutledge Books.*

The last is the *best*!

(4) Last but *not* least, your best option, if you want to produce your memoir in book form, is one I do recommend—*self-publishing.* You are not hiring a commercial printer, and you are not dealing with a royalty publisher or a subsidy publisher. This is known as *independent publishing.* This legitimate option is an increasingly popular and practical way to share your memoir with others in book form. Both professional writers and new writers are doing more self-publishing. It is an honorable route which any writer today may pursue, so your book has no reason to go unpublished. Ways are available for you to produce an attractive, quality book quite economically. This is not a last resort.

The benefits of self-publishing are considerable. You have full control of your production, and it eliminates many middleman expenses. When you sell your books, you keep all profits after actual expenses, and no one pushes you to print more copies than you need. You can order short press runs. You don't need to put out a lot of money for thousands of copies. You do have to make all your own decisions and still pay all the actual expenses. Your biggest job begins after your book is printed because you have to market or distribute it yourself, but with your memoir that should not be a problem. You already know your probable readership.

By self-publishing I mean producing a book either in paperback (trade cover), also called "perfect binding," or hard cover, referred to as "case bound." Some of my books have been published in paperback and some in hardback. I have published with royalty publishers and also self-published.

There are many independent publishers you could research and compare by yourself. I'm going to suggest a short cut based on my personal experience of self-publishing my last ten books with a particular reputable publishing company. They are in business to see writers such as you safely and happily through the entire process. I have no hesitation in unconditionally recommending **Morris Publishing** at 3213 E. Hwy 30, Kearney, NE 68847. Call toll free 800-650-7888, log on to their web site at http://www.morrispublishing.com or e-mail them at: publish@morrispublishing.com.

In *Nebraska?* Yes, and I happily deal with them from Virginia! No problem. I am a satisfied multiple-book customer. They have produced thousands of books for writers in all 50 states.

Because of the completeness and professional quality of their services, I will not use space in this book to walk you through their entire process. They are not a fly-by-night enterprise but have been in the publishing business since 1933. Their prices are lower than most printers because they specialize in standard size 5 ½ x 8 ½ books and offer other excellent standard features so there are some decisions you won't even have to make.

Their distinctiveness is short-run books produced in record time and in quantities of 200 to 5,000 books. This is good news for the memoir writer who doesn't need to put out a large financial outlay for more books than he needs, especially for the first printing. If you need more books, their reprint time is rapid. All phases of the production are done in-house with their own equipment and by skilled and professional staff. That includes graphic design, camera work, printing, binding and shipping.

They don't buy any manuscripts, pay any royalties or market or distribute your books. They print the books professionally and ship them to you. *That's it*. They are not subsidy publishers with hidden or inflated costs. Since you must send them your camera-ready manuscript, you will need to have your book typed and page numbered exactly as you want it. They offer typesetting of Title Pages, Copyright Pages and Mail Order Pages, however. Incredibly, their production time is usually under 45 working days. If cover design assistance is required, they are equipped to do that. Production time is somewhat longer and somewhat more costly, but still economical and rapid.

Here's what to do

Request their no-obligation FREE *Self-publishing*

Package that contains all the information you will need to get started on publishing your memoir or autobiography with them.

The package includes a complete full color *Publishing Guide* with easy to read, no-nonsense price lists, no surprise price adds. Everything is in black and white and up front. The step-by-step *Guide* shows you how to prepare your manuscript and a *Cover Ideas* section offers a selection of no additional cost full color covers where only your title needs to be added. If there is anything they have left unexplained, I don't know what it is. They anticipate your every need. The package includes some sample books they have printed. Contact Morris Publishing for further details as policies may have changed after this printing.

If you plan to offer your book through bookstores too, *Morris Publishing* provides you with complete information and assistance about copyright, an ISBN number, Library of Congress Control Number and bar code. For that they include still another book called *Technical Details*. Those are things about which you don't need to be concerned, however, if you are not producing a book but packaging your life story more informally.

Are you in a hurry? *Morris* has a 25-working-day rush service. An additional charge starts their presses running overtime, without sacrificing the quality.

In the package you will find a free *Marketing Guide* that is worth its weight in gold. You will learn everything you ever wanted to know about self-promoting your book through book signings, interviews, media opportunities, speaking engagements, book reviews, promotional tools and more. When you learn all about producing your book, you will be able to dream realistically.

Now get back to your writing...

I hope you aren't so fired up about the various exciting ways to publish your memoir that you won't finish it! First things first—get to work. You *are* having fun, remember? And when you hold that first copy of your published memoir in your hands, you will feel like you have delivered a baby. You *virtually* have! You lived your life and then *you wrote it!* I'm proud of you because you have left your legacy footprints!

Resources

Some helpful books to aid your memoir writing adventure

Daniel, Lois, *How to Write Your Own Life Story: A Step-by-Step Guide for the Nonprofessional Writer* (Chicago: Chicago Review Press, 1991).

Gibbs, Terri (Editor) *Reflections from a Mother's Heart: A Family Legacy for Your Children* (Dallas: Word Publishing, 1995)

Greene, Bob and Fulford, D.G., *To Our Children's Children: Preserving Family Histories for Generations to Come* (New York: Doubleday, 1993).

Ledbetter, J. Otis and Bruner, Kurt D., *Your Heritage: How to be Intentional About the Legacy You Leave* (Colorado Springs: Victor Books, 1996).

Mungo, Ray, *Your Autobiography: To Help You Write Your Personal History* (New York: Collier Books, 1994).

Polking, Kirk, *Writing Family Histories and Memoirs* (Cincinnati: Betterway Books, 1995).

Lewis, Deborah Shaw and Lewis, Gregg *"Did I Ever Tell You About when Your Grandparents Were Young?"* (Grand Rapids: Zondervan, 1994).

Stanek, Lou Willett, *Writing Your Life: Putting Your Past on Paper*, (New York: Avon Books, 1996).

Thomas, Frank P. *How to Write the Story of Your Life* (Cincinnati: Writer's Digest Books, 1984).

Wiebe, Katie Funk, *Good Times with Old Times: How to Write Your Memoirs* (Scottdale: Herald Press, 1979).

Endnotes

Introduction
1 *Trunk Destiny*—by Leona Choy. Celebrate This Moment. (Winchester, VA: Golden Morning Publishing, 1996) Part 1, p. 17

Chapter 2
1 *Find Us Faithful*—Words and music by Jon Mohr. Copyright 1987 Jonathan Mark Music ASCAP and Birdwing Music ASCAP. All rights reserved.

Page 8
1 *I'm Not a Nobody!*—by Leona Choy. Celebrate This Moment. p. 32

Page 18
1 *Legacy*—by Leona Choy. Celebrate This Moment. p.72

Page 40
1 *My Puzzle*—by Leona Choy. Celebrate This Moment. p.53

Page 60
1 *My Scars*—by Leona Choy. Celebrate This Moment. p. 71

Page 82
1 *Music Score*—by Leona Choy. Celebrate This Moment. p.82

Order the author's autobiography from which she has quoted excerpts in this book.
Contact *Golden Morning Publishing*

About the Author

LEONA CHOY was born of Czech parents in Cedar Rapids, Iowa and graduated from Wheaton College, Illinois. She served with her late husband, Ted, in mission, church, and educational work in Hong Kong, Singapore, China, and the United States.

Leona was a co-founder of *Ambassadors For Christ, Inc.*, a campus ministry among Chinese university students and scholars in North America. Her quarter century of work with AFC was administrative and editorial.

She made 14 trips to the *People's Republic of China* as guide and escort for American travel groups, also ministry trips to Christians in China with her husband, and as an English teaching consultant. More recently she traveled repeatedly to the *Czech Republic* in research for her autobiography published in 2002.

As president of *WTRM-FM* (*Southern Light Gospel Music Network*) in the Shenandoah Valley of Virginia, she produced a daily radio program for five years. She is founder and editorial director of *Golden Morning Publishing* which she established with her son, Rick.

Writer, editor and collaborator of more than 30 books and many foreign language editions, Leona's writing has appeared in scores of periodicals.

Four sons and ten grandchildren keep her busy when she is not at her computer writing more books at her home in Virginia or traveling in speaking ministry.

****

For speaking engagements, reviews of her books, new releases, and book ordering information, contact Leona at:

Golden Morning Publishing
P.O. Box 2697
Winchester, VA 22604

Phone (540) 877-1813
E-mail:
leona@goldenmorning.com
Internet Web Site:
http://www.goldenmorning.com